Mansion on a Hill

The Story of The Willows Maternity
Sanitarium and the Adoption
Hub of America

KelLee Parr

Copyright © 2018 KelLee Parr
All rights reserved.
Printed in USA

For all the young women and their babies who spent time at The Willows

Table of Contents

The Willows Maternity Sanitarium 6
Chapter 1 The Longest Train Ride 7
Chapter 2 Adoption Hub of America 14
Chapter 3 Arriving in Kansas City 25
Chapter 4 The Willows 30
Chapter 5 The "Ritz" 52
Chapter 6 The Mission 67
Chapter 7 Early Years by the Numbers 72
Chapter 8 Life at The Willows 79
Chapter 9 Infamous Adoption at The Willows 91
Chapter 10 Leaving The Willows 95
Chapter 11 Sixty-four Years of Operation 99
Chapter 12 End of an Era 114
Voices of The Willows 118
Chapter 13 Linda's Story 119
Chapter 14 Esther's Story 124
Chapter 15 Sue's Story 131
Chapter 16 Carol's Story 154
Chapter 17 Anita's Story 171
Chapter 18 Phil's Story 176
Chapter 19 Jill's Story 184
Chapter 20 Dyan's Story 203
Chapter 21 Nancy's Story 232
Chapter 22 Danielle's Story 241
Chapter 23 The Rest of Leona's Story 248

Acknowledgments

My family was shaped from the moment my birth grandmother entered The Willows Maternity Sanitarium and when my grandparents traveled to Kansas City to adopt my mother to be a part of their family. I truly appreciate the dedication and tireless work the Haworth family gave to help young women, such as my grandmother, in their difficult time of need. My hope is that this book will help shed some light into the well-hidden role The Willows and other facilities played in the molding of a part of American history kept secret from society.

I wish to thank Carol Haworth Price for her constant support as I strove to learn more about The Willows. The documents, photos and stories Carol provided gave great insight into her family's role in aiding the lives of so many young women and their babies. She helped complete the puzzle of the place of my mother's birth.

Thank you, Margaret Heisserer, for editing and providing friendship and support. I want to thank Rachelle Mengarelli, Sheri Gabbert, LeAnn Harmon, Mark Anselment, and Abel Frederic, who read my drafts and gave valuable feedback, excellent critiques and suggestions for telling The Willows' story. Trista Bieberle once again did an outstanding job creating the cover. Thanks for putting up with all the changes. Debby Williams, thank you for the help with graphics.

I would like to express a special thank you to Skip Keller for colorizing the photo for the cover.

Thank you to Denise Morrison and the Kansas City Museum and Union Station Archives for the photos of the Union Station.

Finally, I want to acknowledge those who shared your Voices of The Willows stories. Linda, Esther, Sue, Carol, Anita, Phil, Jill, Dyan, Nancy and Danielle, thank you for bringing the book to life with your touching stories. I hope what you have shared will encourage others in their searches. A few names have been changed to provide anonymity for certain characters and their families.

As we know, not all reunions turn out to be as positive as the ones shared in this book. And not everyone even has the desire to search, which is perfectly okay. It is my wish that these stories will encourage others still searching not to give up hope. To those who are still trying to decide if they should search, know that finding the answers to the "who" and "why" can be healing.

Part One

The Willows Maternity Sanitarium

While society looked the other way, facilities were established all across America in the first half of the 20th century to help embarrassed and disgraced young, pregnant, unwed women resolve their difficult situations. These women were often whisked away and hidden from society to cover up the transgressions, saving face for the young women and their families. Several months later they returned home. The physical pain and trauma may have subsided, however the emotional wounds never healed.

Kansas City, Missouri, had the distinction of being one of the largest centers for these facilities. This is the story of one of such facilities, perhaps the largest maternity home in the United States, for unwed mothers. The women traveled to Kansas City from all over the country, were kept in seclusion, delivered and gave their babies up for adoption, and then returned home to try to start a new life. The experience was never to be spoken of again. This is the story of The Willows Maternity Sanitarium and the family that owned and operated it, beginning in 1905 until its closing in 1969.

Chapter 1

The Longest Train Ride
(November 17, 1924)

Leona stared in a daze out the window of the Atchison, Topeka and Santa Fe railroad passenger car as it chugged along the track toward its destination, Kansas City, Missouri. It was mid-November and the Kansas prairie foliage had lost its autumn colors due to the frost a few weeks prior. A huge puff of steam from the engine rolled past the thick glass window. It startled her, snapping her out of her trance. Her soul felt dead, just like the brown vegetation on the hillsides out her window.

She bowed her head in despair, glancing at the fabric of her new, blue gingham dress and the polished black-and-white saddle shoes Nick's father, Mr. Belt, bought for her. He said it was just a small gesture to try and reconcile everything. In reality, he just didn't want to be embarrassed by this poor farm girl. She wore her sister Ivy's hand-me-down coat and a simple cloche hat that fit snugly over her dark brunette pageboy. On any other day she would have thought she looked swell – but not today.

Her mind was a quagmire of guilt, shame and fear. Bags under her eyes revealed the nights with no sleep. How had she let this happen? She considered herself such a smart, savvy gal but now a disgrace. A nincompoop to allow herself to be in this situation. As the disgusting boys at school called it "knocked up." Anger and fear boiled in her head. A tear rolled down her cheek, not the first in the past several weeks. Life seemed so unfair. First her papa had died and now this. She was only sixteen years old. Too much for her to handle. She closed her eyes and imagined sitting in the back row of the one-room school house next to her sister Goldie, their little brother Bud at the front of the class. Her teacher, Mr. Martinek, writing math problems on the chalkboard or chiding her for how poorly she'd done on the most recent spelling test. How she wished she were there now.

The loud whistle of the train made her jump. Her brother Louis, sitting next to her, gave a weak smile at her reaction. This was their first experience riding on a locomotive. The two were nervous when they climbed the steps up onto the train from the platform at the small Independence, Kansas, train depot. Louis went first and Leona took his hand and the conductor's hand as they lifted her up onto the first step. Louis led her past rows of men, women, and children already boarded, heading for the metropolis of Kansas City. The train was abuzz with activity and voices. They found two empty seats, and Leona took the window seat. She felt protected by her older brother. He blocked the imagined glares of the other passengers.

Leona thought he looked dapper dressed in his best Sunday clothes and their father's black fedora hat. He appeared much older than his twenty years. Normally, a first train ride would be exhilarating – but not for Leona. The only thing that made it tolerable was Louis' calming presence.

A smartly dressed man in his late twenties and his attractive young wife sat across facing Leona and Louis. The couple beamed with pride as the new mother cradled a small baby wrapped in a pink blanket. A beautifully crocheted white cap rested on the baby's head. Leona watched the woman clutch her sleeping daughter and felt her own heart tighten. Though she never made eye contact, Leona sensed stares of disapproval. She wrapped her arms tighter around her growing, yet still unnoticeable, belly to hide her shame. Her heart broke, thinking of Nick and their baby. Would their baby be a boy or girl? Would Nick even care enough to know? Leona turned her face away, certain her dream of a family like this one would never be reality.

The train steamed its way northeast. Leona kept her head down. She leaned against her big brother, avoiding interaction with the family sitting across from her. She closed her eyes and rested her head on his broad shoulder. Louis was Leona's rock through this whole messy ordeal. She knew how embarrassed and disappointed he was in her, but he would never say it. His chiseled, clenched jaw and lack of a smile told her he was distraught and worried. She knew his world was as disarrayed as hers by her past actions.

Louis returned home after the news broke that changed their family dynamics. Run off by their envious and cruel stepfather, Louis had left their farm to find work in a nearby town. After hearing of Leona's pregnancy, the pompous stepfather dropped out of the picture, and Louis came home to take over as man of the house. She didn't know what would have happened if he hadn't returned. It was Louis who helped console her and confront Nick and Mr. Belt.

Exhausted, Leona began to drift off to sleep. As she dozed, she relived the events that brought her here. The swaying of the train made her feel as if she was once again dancing with the most handsome fella' she had ever seen. How special Nick made her feel! She enjoyed the touch of his arms around her. She heard him saying he loved her. She began to relive the intimate details of that special moment, but her dream turned dark. The recurring nightmare began. Louis in the buggy taking her to Mr. Belt's farm. Louis stepping onto the front porch as Mr. Belt came to the door. The raised voices when Nick came out of the house. Mr. Belt slapping Nick upside the head. The slam of the door as Nick ran back into the house. Louis turning with a sour look on his face and making the long walk to the buggy. Her despair when he said that Nick had just gotten married and his wife was pregnant. Leona's dream shattered. She made a slight whimper and jerked in her sleep, waking herself. Louis pulled his baby sister in tighter, aware of the pain she was suffering.

She and Louis left before sunup to make the trip to the Independence train depot with Mr. Belt. Mama cried, giving her sweet "Ona" a hug as she handed her daughter over to Mr. Belt. As part of their agreement, he took care of all the financial arrangements. This was only the second time Leona had seen the man. He was every bit as scary and imposing as the day she saw him hit Nick when Louis delivered the news of her pregnancy.

Mr. Belt was at least six foot two and a muscular man from his life of farm work. His thick, gray, slick-backed hair was parted down the middle. His bushy, handlebar mustache and cold, dark eyes gave him an intimidating presence. The first time Leona saw him he wore new, dark blue overalls that were his church clothes, typical Sunday farmer apparel. But today he looked like a businessman in his gray dress suit and matching fedora hat. He looked very rich and dignified, much like the town's banker always appeared. A big, fat smoldering cigar hung from his mouth.

When Mr. Belt picked them up at their house in his black Model T, Leona wondered if Nick would come, too. She should have known he wouldn't. In any other situation, Leona's excitement for her first ride in a horseless carriage couldn't have been contained but not today.

"Mr. Belt is a very rich man," Louis whispered in her ear.

The Model T had isinglass windows along the side to try and keep out the cold November air. Thankfully Mama sent with her a handmade, ruby-red and brown tweed lap blanket to help keep her warm. She also sent some homemade bread, cheese, salami, and apples for them to eat on the trip, not that Leona had an appetite. Louis opened the passenger door so Leona could crawl into the back seat while he sat down in the front seat.

MANSION ON A HILL

 Mr. Belt cranked the car engine, and it roared to life. Leona was scared to death as the motorcar shook and shimmied. It sure wasn't the first automobile ride she had envisioned months ago with Nick driving and taking her down Main Street while she waved at her friends as they passed by.
 The ride to the train station was a little under twenty miles. With Mr. Belt's pride and joy clipping along the old dirt road at a good pace, it only took an hour and half. Mr. Belt was gruff and didn't seem any too pleased with his passengers. Louis and he exchanged a few idle comments. The elder man told Louis he had a letter with instructions for when Louis and Leona arrived in Kansas City. This information brought any conversation to a silent halt. Mr. Belt puffed on his cigar and guided the bouncing carriage down the bumpy road.
 The nasty smoke plus the motion from riding in the back seat of the car made Leona nauseous. She fought it for several miles, but it became too much. "Stop, let me out," Leona pleaded. "I am going to be sick."
 Mr. Belt pulled over and let a few curse words fly. "Don't you be gettin' sick in my new Model T!" he bellowed.
 Louis jumped out allowing Leona to scramble out of the back seat just in time to throw up by the side of the road. It was not the best idea for Leona to have eaten the big breakfast of bacon, eggs, and biscuits Mama fixed and insisted she eat. Louis steadied her, holding her hair out of her face while she emptied the contents of her stomach. She felt as if she was about to slip into unconsciousness from exhaustion as she continued to heave. Slowly her body calmed, and she decided she was not going to die.
 "Sis, are you okay?" Louis asked.
 She wiped her lips with the back of her hand and frowned at the terrible taste left in her mouth. She was mortified. She did not want to ride in that automobile again! She nodded she was okay. With disgust in his voice, Mr. Belt ordered the two to get in the car or they would be late for the train. Louis helped Leona climb in and crawled

into the backseat with her this time. He covered her with the lap blanket and put his arm around her. Leona wrapped her arms tightly across her body, closed her eyes, and willed herself not to get sick again. Other than the roar of the engine, there was silence the rest of the way to the train depot.

When they got to the depot, Leona was never so glad to feel the ground beneath her feet. Louis wrapped the blanket around her shoulders, and the two walked to the train platform. Mr. Belt headed for the ticket office to buy the tickets for them. Louis carried Leona's small clothes bag and sack with the food Mama had sent. He put his free arm around her waist. Leona shivered not only from the cold but with fear of what lay ahead. Mr. Belt joined the pair after he purchased the tickets but stood with his back toward them, as if he didn't recognize them. He puffed on his putrid cigar as they stood in solemn quiet, waiting for the train to arrive.

Others were chatting and laughing in anticipation of the exciting train ride. The train whistle could be heard from miles away as it approached. A young boy chased his little sister as she squealed in glee. The mother scolded the two to come to her and stand still. Leona felt empty as they waited for the journey in front of them.

After a few minutes, which seemed like an eternity to Leona, the ominous black train with its engine puffing white smoke and pulling passenger cars lined with window after window came into sight. It slowly pulled up to the platform and came to a stop. The conductor stuck his head out the doorway and began helping the few passengers step down who were disembarking. If passengers had luggage, he would carry it down and place it at the bottom of the steps on the platform. Once the train was deboarded, the conductor yelled, "All aboard!"

The waiting passengers started pushing toward the steps. The family with the young boy and girl were at the front of the line. Mr. Belt handed Louis the tickets and a letter then nodded at him without saying a word. Leona kept her head down. She couldn't look the man in the eyes. The moment they stepped onto the train and Mr. Belt was assured the "problem" was being removed, he turned and walked to his fancy automobile. His grimace turned to a slight smile as he knew the humiliating situation was taken care of for good.

As the train pulled from the depot, Leona was on her way to a place Mr. Belt called The Willows Maternity Sanitarium. He said it was the finest "home" for young women in the country. It sounded like a dreadful place to Leona. This was her first time to ever be away from her mama. She felt the early pangs of homesickness, but maybe the morning sickness was returning. The first few months of her pregnancy were hell. Then again, maybe this was motion sickness similar to her experience earlier in the day. Likely a combination of all three. Whatever the cause, she felt nauseous. Looking out the window any length of time seemed to only make things worse. She felt dizzy as the countryside sped by. She told herself she could not get sick again and not on the train. She would not draw more attention and embarrassment for Louis's sake. She fought back the physical effects her body felt from the train ride, giving thanks her breakfast was long gone. The train moved onward to their destination, stopping at every small town along the way to pick up passengers. She kept her eyes closed, her head resting on Louis's shoulder, in silence.

Leona, July 4, 1924

Chapter 2

Adoption Hub of America

Leona and Louis journeyed closer to their stop at the Kansas City Union Station depot and her new temporary home, The Willows. She was petrified. She felt as if she was being punished and banished for the sins of her indiscretion. She was certain no person ever hated their first train ride as much as she did. Little did she know how wrong she was.

Hundreds of thousands before and after Leona experienced the same anguish and despair that she felt on her first train ride in 1924. Starting in about 1854, a first large wave of humanity was shipped by train to Kansas City and other Midwest locales. These were scared, young, orphaned children from large, east coast cities, especially New York City and Boston.

Orphanages overflowed onto the streets of the cities' slums. Some children were orphaned when their parents died in epidemics of tuberculosis, typhoid, yellow fever or the flu. Others were abandoned due to poverty, illness or addiction. A man named Charles Loring Brace helped organize the Children's Aid Society to help these impoverished orphans to be sent by train to the Midwest cities and towns where families were looking to adopt children, often to be laborers to support their new families' farms. It is estimated that from 1854 until 1929 up to 250,000 orphans rode the rails west on what later became known as the orphan trains.[1] Stories, both good and bad, are plentiful about the lives of these orphan train children. The impact of the orphan trains on our nation is well documented in American history through books and movies. There is even a National Orphan Train Museum and Research Center located in Concordia, Kansas.

Few people are aware of a secretive second wave of humanity that traveled to Kansas City, Missouri, starting in the early 1900s. Trains—and in later years cars and planes—brought over 100,000 scared, young women in the same predicament as Leona to Kansas City. Leona's baby was just one of thousands of babies born and left to be adopted in Kansas City. However, unlike the orphan trains, this historical phenomenon is not well-known or well-documented.

In the early to mid-1900s, mortified, pregnant, unwed girls often went away to "visit distant relatives" for a few months, give birth to their babies and return home as if nothing had happened – their secret hidden from society, though often providing whispered gossip and embarrassment. Many of these girls were sent by train to facilities such as The Willows Maternity Sanitarium. The girls gave up their newborns for adoption, often with no say in the matter, hoping to purge their families' humiliation and disgrace.

Society looked down on these young, unmarried women who found themselves pregnant. Being "in the family way" and unwed was a mortal sin. It ruined the reputation of the girl. It was totally unacceptable for a respectable girl to be sexually active. Of course, not all the pregnancies were from consensual sex. Many of the young girls and women were sexual assault victims, but in those days, rape was considered the fault of the victim. Society often ignored the source of the unwed mother's pregnancy. Scrutiny was placed on the pregnant girl no matter the circumstances. Society and religious circles ostracized these girls. No self-respecting man would consider marrying a woman who had born a child out of wedlock, especially if the child belonged to another man. A woman's entire life could be destroyed if her secret was revealed. It could lead to becoming condemned, a lonely outcast and poverty stricken, while forcing some women, including teenage girls, into prostitution.

Not only was the young woman considered to be immoral and "damaged goods," but the respectability and morality of her family was called into question. Hypocritically, society didn't seem to have as much of an issue with the young man involved, but his family's reputation and humiliation was often a matter of concern. This sometimes led to the birth father's family, especially wealthier ones with higher stakes in society, helping to pay the girl's way, wanting to see the situation kept secret and swept under the rug.

Facilities for unwed mothers popped up all over the country in the early 1900s. The Willows was just one of several such Kansas City facilities all located within walking distance or a short taxi ride from the Union Station railroad depot. The Willows took on the mission to help these young women and provide seclusion from the judgmental scrutiny of society. Other facilities were the Fairmount Maternity Hospital, Fairmount Eastside Maternity Hospital (later known as the Kansas City Cradle), St. Vincent's Hospital, and the Florence Crittenton Homes.

Florence Crittenton Homes were first established in New York City in 1883 as a refuge for outcast women and girls. It was often noted that the unfortunate girls who couldn't afford to pay for their confinement and care were usually referred to the Crittenton Home. Those who entered the other hospitals were for the most part girls and women from more prosperous family backgrounds. In the early days in Kansas City, there were two Florence Crittenton facilities, the Florence Crittenton Hospital and the Florence Crittenton Home for Colored Girls. For over a century, their facilities across the United States provided services for young women, and they continue to fulfill their mission to this day.

Beginning in 1905, it is estimated The Willows saw over 35,000 young women revolve through its doors until its closing in 1969. As astonishing as those numbers are, it was just a portion of the even more staggering number of teenage girls and women who sought sanctuary in Kansas City, Missouri. Well over 100,000 young, unwed women in the "family way" traveled, mostly by train, to Kansas City from all over the United States and even other countries to deliver their babies in anonymity. The professional adoption sector in the early 1900s dubbed Kansas City the "Adoption Hub of America." In 1925, the year Leona gave birth, The Willows was the temporary residence for 344 girls from forty of the forty-eight states as well as Canada and the Hawaiian Islands.

A July 2, 1950, post from the north Kansas City newspaper, *The Sun Tribune*, shows the continuation of the concept of the "Adoption Hub of America" well into the 1950s.

> *The adoption court in Kansas City places about 1,000 babies a year, thus making it one of the largest and possibly THE largest child placement agency in America. In contrast to the scores of orphanages, maternity homes, hospitals and other institutions or homes from which children may be adopted in most cities, Kansas City has only four. They are the Eastside, Fairmount, and Willows hospitals—maternity homes exclusively for unwed mothers; and the Florence Crittenton Home for Infants.*[2]

Today there are still facilities for unwed, pregnant girls across the United States, but most of the larger homes or hospitals, such as The Willows Maternity Sanitarium, closed in the late 1960s and 70s when societal norms of the day began to change. Events such as the anti-Vietnam War movement (Make Love, Not War), the 60s sexual revolution, birth control pills, and Roe v. Wade in 1973 changed the demand for such homes for unwed girls.

There were four contributing factors that made Kansas City, Missouri, a prime destination for pregnant, unwed girls to go to have their babies and young couples to seek babies to adopt. First, being close to the geometrical center of the contiguous United States, it was easy to reach Kansas City from all areas of the country. In the beginning years of The Willows, most of the young women were from the surrounding states of Missouri, Kansas, Iowa, and Nebraska. The Willows' numbers quickly expanded to other states due to a second factor.

The train system had a huge impact in making Kansas City the "Adoption Hub of America" and was the second factor. Trains from all over the country arrived in Kansas City, and it became one of the most important centers for travel.

KANSAS CITY AS A RAILROAD CENTER

"Who Enter Here Find Quiet and Peace and Rest" Map 1925[3]
After the old Union Depot was flooded and destroyed in 1903, a new Union Station was built on higher ground. It opened on October 30, 1914, close to the bluffs overlooking downtown Kansas City. It was the second largest train station in the United States. Over 670,000 people passed through its doors in 1945 at the peak of its passenger traffic. Imagine the unfathomable feelings of a young pregnant girl, often traveling alone, when she entered such a mammoth facility with the hustle

and bustle of the throngs of humanity from all walks of life. In contrast, picture the nervous but excited young couple arriving by train to adopt their first child and return home with their baby to love and nurture.

Photos of the Kansas City Union Station in mid-1920s
Courtesy of the Kansas City Museum and Union Station Archives, Kansas City, MO

The third factor was the simplified adoption system. Missouri courts made it easy to adopt. In the early days, it was possible for couples to come to Kansas City in the morning, sign the court papers and take a baby home later that day. A few months later the official adoption would be finalized.

Before 1917, the State of Missouri required adoptions to be filed by deed in the county of residence of the person adopting the child. After 1917, adoptions in Missouri required a petition to be filed in the juvenile division of the circuit court of either the county where the child resided or the county where the person seeking to adopt resided. All the babies from The Willows were placed through the Jackson County Circuit Courts. When prospective parents applied for adoption of an infant, they received an "adopted" or amended birth certificate with the child's new chosen name and names of the adoptive parents as the official parents. Adoptive parents did not see or receive the original birth certificates for their adopted children.

The July 2, 1950, post from *The Sun Tribune* explained how efficient the adoption court system in Kansas City was. It also shared the emphasis placed on finding good families for the adoptees. They wanted homes that were financially secure and church-going couples.

> *Any applications that are sent direct to the maternity homes are automatically referred to the adoption department of the Juvenile court. The court's own caseworkers make all the investigations and recommendations for placement. There is only one adoption agency (the court) one adoption judge (Ray G. Cowan), and one adoption director (Mary Lou Fenberg) whose recommendation to Judge Cowan is required in every adoption proceeding. There are 15 staff members under Mrs. Fenberg who are assigned to the adoption office to interview adoptive parents and unwed mothers. The others are full time case workers who are assigned to the four maternity hospitals to*

investigate the backgrounds of both the mothers and fathers of the illegitimate children, and to check on the health and physical development of the babies. The Kansas City adoption court has become nationally famous for its job of matching babies to parents.

Qualifications for adoptive parents are high. The theory is that with nearly 100 applicants for every available baby, the agency can be choosy. Wealth is not a prerequisite, though the court requires that applicants offer proof of enough financial security to provide comfortable standards of living and education for the child. Also, couples who want a Kansas City baby must be regular church goers. Just belonging to a church isn't enough.

Lastly, an even more important factor was the discretion Missouri adoption laws provided the families. Some estimates show in the 1900s through the 1960s as many as 400,000 to 500,000 adoptions took place in Missouri with about 100,000 in Kansas City alone. Missouri's stringent closed adoptions provided privacy for both biological parents and adoptive parents. All birth records and original birth certificates (OBC) were permanently sealed, assuring anonymity and to hide the secret for the birth mother and father. Quite often the birth father's name was not even recorded on the OBC. It assured birth parents that the child could not get their information if the child ever did want to search for them.

Adoptive parents chose Kansas City, coming from all parts of the country to Missouri to adopt, because the state's laws assured secrecy with no concern of birth parents changing their minds and being able to find their babies. In the early years, the girls were often told they should not search for their babies. In 1925, Leona was told she should never look for her baby to ensure her baby's life was not interrupted, and Leona never did look. In the 50s and 60s, girls were informed they had up to six months to change their minds and claim their babies before the adoption was final. It was a rare situation when this happened. It should be noted that quite often it wasn't the girl who wanted the secrecy but was for her parents' privacy and for them to save face. In Leona's case, it was to provide protection of the father's reputation. Many girls in this situation were trapped. Though most girls might prefer to keep their babies, they had no choice but to sign over their babies for adoption. Leona wanted to keep her baby but, as a seventeen-year-old unmarried woman, that wasn't an option. At the time of birth, the mothers could include some health information or write letters to leave in their children's files even though these records were sealed. In later years this non-disclosure information was able to be retrieved from county records upon request by the adopted child.

A 1924 thirty-two-page brochure for doctors titled "Finesse of Service: Explaining to Our Physician Patrons Some of the Refinements in Our Plans for the Protection of Their Unfortunate Patients" lays out all the details and philosophy of The Willows in providing this privacy for their clients. One section with the heading "Protect Mother and Child Against Each Other" assures the protection of identity of mother and child, as well as the inconspicuous father. It reads:

> It is the studied effort of the Management of The Willows in its various departments to protect the unfortunate mother against the possibility of her child later becoming an impediment to her success and future. In fact, the proper service of a seclusion maternity sanitarium is a two-fold protection: that of protecting the mother against the child and the people who adopt it, and that of protecting the child and its foster parents against the mother and her friends.[4]

Adopted children often want to learn about their birth parents, their heritage and health issues. It was very difficult searching for information for adoptees born in Missouri, as is still true in many states. In the past, some people were able to gain access to some of the information in their adoption files by using search agents or "angels." Search angels are people, often adoptees themselves, who help adoptees look for birth parents. A state agency will sometimes allow these search angels to have access to the closed files, but the search agent cannot disclose any of the information to the adoptee. A search angel often locates a birth parent from the information gleaned from the file and asks if he or she wants to be contacted by the adopted child. If the birth parent agrees, the adopted child is given the contact information and the reunion made. Search angels have helped innumerable adoptees find their birth parents.

Over the years, many attempts were made to change access to birth records in Missouri. One example was in 1980 when the Model Adoption Act was brought before the Missouri State Congress. It tried to change the procedure of placement of adoptees from licensed child care placing agencies to unlicensed intermediaries. It also would have given access to original birth certificates (OBCs) to adoptees. There were many who fought for and against this legislation. It did not pass.

In 2011, Missouri adoption laws were changed, allowing adoptees whose biological parents were deceased to request and receive their adoption files from the court where their adoption took place. Previously those records remained sealed even after the death of the biological parents. Disclosure of names was allowed only if the birth parent was known to be deceased. If the birth parent was alive and could be reached, permission had to be granted before the child received information. This prevented many adoptees from locating birth parents.

Adoption rights advocates fought many years to get the records unsealed. It was not until 2016 that the Missouri laws changed again thanks to the submission and passage of a bill sponsored by Missouri State Representative Don Phillips, himself an adoptee, that allowed adopted children to legally obtain their original birth certificates

(OBC) with birth parents' names. This was a huge win for adoptees wishing to glean information about their heritage and birth. Anyone born before 1941 could get their OBC after August 28, 2016. Those born after January 1, 1941, would have to wait until January 1, 2018, to be able to get their OBC. Additional changes to the law were made in June of 2018 when the Missouri governor signed into law a bill allowing children and direct descendants to see the OBC of a deceased parent who was adopted.

Chapter 3

Arriving in Kansas City

Obviously, Mr. Belt was made aware of the Missouri laws in 1924 that protected his family from anyone ever knowing about this unwanted baby or his son's imprudent behavior. After finding out about Leona's pregnancy, Mr. Belt consulted with the local doctor. The doctor remembered receiving a ninety-page catalogue advertising The Willows Maternity Sanitarium, their services, and the privacy they promised. He shared this information with Mr. Belt noting The Willows was possibly the perfect solution for his dilemma.

The Willows Maternity Sanitarium Catalogue from 1917[5]

The "little problem" was whisked away by train 175 miles to Kansas City. When Leona and Louis finally arrived at the Union Station, they deboarded the train. Neither of them had ever seen anything so amazing or grand in their entire lives. The gigantic stone building was breathtaking. It made the tall corn silo on the Belt farm look like one of Mama's thimbles by comparison. Even the biggest buildings in Independence now seemed miniscule. People were scurrying about in every direction as trains arrived and departed. The two siblings locked arms as they made their way through the huge doors of the entrance to the building.

Once inside, Louis pulled out Mr. Belt's instructions. He practically had them memorized from reading the letter over and over during the train ride. The piece of paper was stationery with a photo of two babies at the top and a heading that read "The Willows Maternity Sanitarium." The letter had been written to Mr. Belt with instructions on which train to catch and departure time. It was written by a Mrs. Nellie McEwen who noted a woman would be there waiting for the "young girl Leona" at the Union Station. Her name was Mrs. Reed. She was a nurse who worked at The Willows. She would have on a white dress and white nurse's cap. She had short, dark hair and glasses. She would be waiting for them by the main south entrance of the building. If they had any trouble, they were to ask a Union Station worker where the south entrance was located.

Louis and Leona navigated through the crowd of people, dodging suitcases and elbows as they made their way to the center of the cavernous room. Normally finding directions would be a cinch for Louis but with no sun to direct him and all these jostling people, he was totally turned around. He saw a sign that said "Information" and a podium surrounded by lots of folks talking to a man. They stopped and waited their turn to ask the harried man at the podium where they would find the south entrance. The worker smiled and pointed to the huge doors on the opposite wall from where they had entered. Louis thanked the man and held Leona close as the two headed in that direction. Leona kept the folded lap blanket over her arm, hiding her belly. Louis carried her small bag and the still uneaten provisions their mother had sent. As they reached the big doors, they saw a woman standing alone wearing a black cape with white skirt showing below. The white, pointed nurse's cap on her head and glasses provided the clues they needed as they approached her.

Louis addressed the stranger, asking if she was Nurse Reed. She acknowledged that yes indeed she was and asked if this was Leona. Leona looked up and tried to smile as she nodded yes. Louis introduced himself and thanked her for meeting them. Nurse Reed in turn thanked Louis for accompanying Leona and dismissed him to return home on the train. Leona clung to her brother's arm and did not want to let go. Her eyes begged him to stay. With concern and disbelief in his voice, he said to Nurse Reed, "I figured I would go with her all the way to make sure she settles in okay."

Nurse Reed gave him a warm smile and said, "It is better if you don't come with us to The Willows. It is very private and, for the sake of the other girls, not appropriate for family members to be at the house. You need to head back home. The next train to Independence leaves in about thirty minutes. Here is your ticket. You leave at Gate 3."

She handed Louis the prearranged ticket Mr. Belt had paid for and told the two siblings they needed to say their goodbyes. Louis sadly gave Leona a long hug. A tear rolled down Leona's cheek. Louis, with watering eyes, pulled her clinging limbs off from around him and took her chin in his hand, making her look up. He smiled saying, "Sis, all will be okay."

Nurse Reed placed her hand on Leona's shoulder. She turned Leona toward her and away from Louis. Taking hold of Leona's hand, Nurse Reed wished Louis safe travels and bade him goodbye as she pulled Leona in the direction of the gaping door. Leona looked back forlornly over her shoulder at Louis. He stood dumbstruck, watching this stranger lead his baby sister out the exit of the station then disappear from view. His heart sank, knowing he could not protect her anymore. He wondered if he would ever see his little sister again.

Outside the Union Station, Nurse Reed hailed a taxi. The driver pulled up to the curb and jumped out, coming around the rear of the motorcar to open the door for Leona and Nurse Reed. This would be Leona's second automobile ride in just one day, and the two climbed into the back seat. Nurse Reed assured Leona all would be just fine, and she would love staying at The Willows. It was a wonderful place. The other girls and the staff were all very nice. Nurse Reed asked the driver to take them to 2929 Main Street, and the driver – with a smirk on his face – pulled the taxi out away from the curb. The driver turned right onto the busy street, and Leona noticed the street sign said Main Street. They headed up a steep hill. At the top of the hill, the driver made a U-turn. The cab pulled up along beside the sidewalk and stopped. The ride took only a quick minute or two.

Leona felt disoriented and everything seemed a blur. All seemed to be happening so fast. Nurse Reed was being cordial but very businesslike as she paid the fare to the taxi driver. He jumped out and came around to open their door. The two got out of the taxi, and Leona looked at the stairsteps going up to an enormous, red brick building partially hidden behind large trees. Leona would never forget the long climb from the street up the steep steps on the hillside. She carried her meager possessions toward the ominous mansion sitting on the hill. At the top of steps that seemed to go on forever was the entrance with a beautiful wooden, columned pergola. A sign read "The Willows Hospital." Rose vines blanketed the pergola, providing shade in the summer and protection from the cold in the winter. It gave her an eerie feeling as if walking into a whole new world. Girls often felt as if they were walking in a tunnel as they approached the front door. The brick building had huge ornate pillars on each side of the stairs leading to the wooden door.

MANSION ON A HILL

A Mansion on a Hill in 1925
Photo courtesy of Carol Haworth Price

Leona never saw anything so grand as The Willows, not even the rich banker's house back home could compare. This would be Leona's secluded home for the next several months. She climbed the steps with Nurse Reed and entered the building, feeling completely overwhelmed in this new world.

Chapter 4

The Willows

The Willows Maternity Sanitarium in 1909[6]

The Willows Maternity Sanitarium was an anomaly amongst the mansions lining the bluff overlooking Main Street of Kansas City, Missouri. Homes owned by some of the earliest, wealthy families in the city were built along the crest of this large hill because of the panoramic view it provided of the sprawling city. The huge structure was built in 1873 by Asa Maddox for his family. Maddox was a Kansas City pioneer lumberman, who had no idea he was building the future "home" for thousands of young women to be hidden from the world because of their unfortunate situations. The mansion was purchased in 1908 by Edwin and Cora May Haworth (pronounced Hah-worth). It included five acres from the original tract on which the house was built.

Cora May Haworth and Edwin Pearl (E.P.) Haworth
Photos courtesy of Carol Haworth Price

The Haworths purchased the building with the intention of turning it into a refuge for young, unwed mothers. They actually started helping girls in 1905 when a family friend's daughter found herself pregnant and unmarried. The girl's family confided in the Haworths and said they intended to send her away to relatives until after the birth of her child to alleviate the embarrassment of the situation. Mrs. Haworth told the family that the girl should come stay with them instead, and they would look after her and the baby. They helped the girl to place her baby for adoption. The Haworths realized there were other young women in the same situation. They took in two or three more girls and made it their life goal to help others. Three years after taking in this first young lady, they purchased the Maddox mansion and The Willows Maternity Sanitarium was born.

The Willows got off to a rough start after the Maddox mansion was converted into the maternity hospital. After opening earlier in the year of 1908, the Haworth's dream almost came to a quick ending. On December 24, Christmas Eve morning, there were twenty young women and nine infants in the building, as well as seven nurses and Mr. and Mrs. Haworth. Most of them were asleep when one of the nurses smelled smoke coming from the attic. She proceeded to wake everyone, and they called the fire department. According to an article from *The Kansas City Star* newspaper dated December 24, 1908:

> *Six women were carried out by firemen. Mr. Haworth, aided by neighbors, carried out all of the babies first. The infants and their mothers were taken to another house, an annex of the hospital.*
>
> *The cause of the fire was not determined by Edward Trickett, fire warden, who made an investigation. It started in the northwest corner of the attic, where several mattresses stuffed with excelsior were stored. Mice and matches was the theory of Alexander Henderson, assistant fire chief.*[7]

The roof was badly burned, and the upper part of the house severely damaged. Thankfully, all the residents were safe, and the building was restored to use.

Advertising the new business became essential to the success of The Willows. The Haworths advertised their facility in medical journals and reviews across the country in the 1910s and 1920s. The ads emphasized the sanitarium provided seclusion and privacy. Below is one of the earliest ads, placed in the *Medical Review* in 1907 before The Willows Sanitarium Hospital at 2929 Main Street was in operation. The Haworth's granddaughter Carol Haworth Price said the house shown in the ad at 217 Park Ave is not her grandparents' home. Her best guess is it was a picture used to keep people from recognizing their house and going there to find someone.

1907 *Medical Review* Ad[8]

The advertisement goes into great detail to explain the services provided. It states:

> *A Sanitarium Home especially adapted to the care of* **Unfortunate Girls and Women who wish to avoid Publicity.** *Cases not requiring seclusion also taken.*

> *The sanitarium furnishes strictly modern home comforts, home life and home privileges and is liberally equipped with apparatus for obstetric work. Patients may enter and be in retirement for as long before confinement as they desire. Each is taught to prepare for sickness while in waiting. Child adopted if desired.*

> *Light, airy, comfortable rooms; new furnishings and equipment; palatable and nourishing food; modern sanitary conveniences, elevating influences and good moral atmosphere.*

"They wanted the young women and their babies to have the very best care they could possibly have," shared the Haworth's granddaughter. "Expenses were not spared there. They ate well. They had fabulous cooks who cooked for them. All of the equipment was updated as often as one could update equipment. They found loving homes for the babies through doctors who would give recommendations to adoptive parents. These doctors knew of The Willows and the kind of care these infants received, plus the prenatal care that the birth mothers had received was so good."

It was imperative to the success of The Willows for the Haworths in their advertising to state their philosophy and share their mission to help young women. In the 1930 document titled "A Ten Years' Survey of Seclusion Maternity Service: A Sociological Analysis of the Patients Cared for by The Willows Maternity Sanitarium Covering the Ten-year Period, 1920–1929 Inclusive," Mr. Haworth writes:

> *The Willows Maternity Sanitarium is humanitarian in its work and for the past twenty years has been caring for one class of unfortunates to whom society has been less kind than to any other of her offspring – the unfortunate young woman. Twenty years of successful service in seclusion maternity work is adequate proof to those who have questioned the advisability of rendering such services to unfortunate young women, that it is a worthy and necessary service and not only are the patients and their families benefited, but it is a decided step forward in the emancipation of women from the old idea that such a misfortune must be endured for all eternity and the unfortunate one left to the mercy of gossip and a heartless world.*[9]

Mr. Haworth created copious documents and advertisements throughout the early years of The Willows to spread the news. His genius in marketing was apparent by their success. He started *The Wil-*

lows Magazine, publishing the first issue in November, 1911. The magazine was bi-monthly and distributed to over 16,700 physicians across Missouri, Kansas, Iowa, Nebraska, Oklahoma, and parts of Arkansas and Texas. He targeted physicians with his advertisements, knowing they would most likely be the contact person for the girls in the difficult predicament of being an unwed mother with nowhere to turn. The magazine was also a way to recruit nurses to work at the hospital.

Showing his love and skill for writing, in 1917 and 1918 Mr. Haworth wrote two intriguing, fictional documents to share with doctors who might be seeking services for pregnant, unmarried girls. The document from 1917 was titled "My Diary—by Elizabeth." It starts by sharing the entries of a fictitious Willows' patient named Elizabeth and includes drawings.

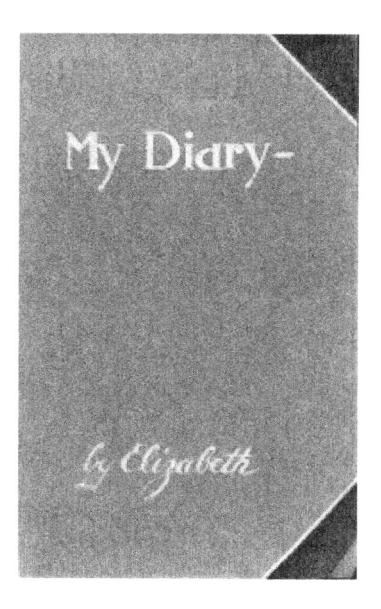

1917 Document "My Diary—by Elizabeth"[10]

KELLEE PARR

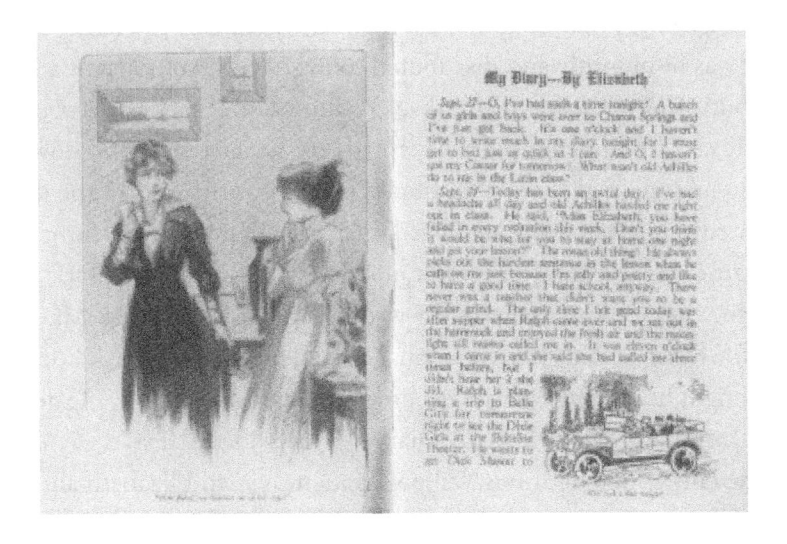

The diary describes the perils of a young girl who finds herself pregnant with her boyfriend Ralph's baby. She is mortified by the embarrassment it has brought upon her family. The detailed account of what Elizabeth experiences at The Willows is very positive and upbeat written from Mr. Haworth's biased viewpoint. However, it does give a very detailed and captivating look into the daily operation of the facility not found elsewhere. It is interesting to note that when a girl was about to give birth, the girl is said to be "sick." These are some of the entries in the diary.

> Sept. 27 – O, I've had such a time tonight! A bunch of us girls and boys went over to Charon Springs and I've just got back. It's one o'clock and I haven't time to write much in my diary tonight for I must get to bed just as quick as I can.

> Sept. 30 – It was too late to write any when I got home last night. As it is Saturday I've been in bed almost all day trying to catch up sleep for we are going to have a moonlight picnic tonight out at Bunker's Grove. Miss Burg is going along to

MANSION ON A HILL

chaperon. I hate Miss Burg – sour old maid – never had a beau in her life, I'll bet!

I hate Ralph this evening.

Oct. 16 – I've been so busy I just haven't been able to find time to keep up my diary. Ralph and I took a long hike out to the old mill tonight after school. This October weather is simply wonderful. I hate to think of school again tomorrow. I wish I could go away with Ralph to some desert island where there would be no one but just us two and stay forever. Education wouldn't be necessary there.

Nov. 30 – I don't feel one bit good tonight and I have hunted up my old diary again. I really think I'll feel better to write it all down and get it out of my system before I try to go to sleep. Yesterday was Thanksgiving and I must have eaten too much. At least I was sick this morning and vomited terribly. I haven't been feeling like myself for a month and mama has been worried about me continually. I wish she'd forget it. Today she wanted to take me to see the doctor, but I told her I did not feel able to go. Then I had an awful time keeping her from calling him here, and I only kept her from it by promising that I would go with her to his office tomorrow. I'll have to get out of *it somehow again. I don't want to go because I'm afraid to. I'm afraid – O, I wish I could see Ralph and talk to him a little bit tonight.*

Dec. 1 – I saw Ralph this evening. I told him how scared I am and he is scared, too. I am almost sure – O, I can't write it, but I am sure of it and I don't know what in the world to do. Ralph comforted me and told me not to worry as he was sure everything would come out all right. He is going to see Dr. Harrison himself tomorrow and get me some medicine and no one, not even mama, ever need to know anything about it.

Dec. 2 – I saw Ralph again tonight and, believe me, he is a scared kid. I don't know what Dr. Harrison said to him, but it must have been something awful. And he didn't get any medicine either. Ralph never told him it was me. I admire Ralph's sense of honor. He certainly is a gentleman! But I think he might have succeeded if he had just told everything to the doctor. Ralph says it is useless for him to go back, but I am sure Dr. Harrison would not have refused to do anything if he had known it was me. I've made up my mind to go and see him myself tomorrow. It is getting to be a serious matter and something has got to be done and done right away.

MANSION ON A HILL

The next day the doctor tells Elizabeth there is nothing he can do without examining her, and she must bring her mother back with her to visit him. She is scared to tell her mother, but the next morning she shares her fear. Elizabeth is shocked at her mother's reaction. Her mother is furious and calls Elizabeth all kinds of names. Elizabeth's father hears the commotion and discovers the problem at hand. He has a calmer head, and that afternoon he is the one to take his daughter back to see the doctor.

> Dec. 4 – Doctor Harrison said I was two months pregnant. Poor father! His eyes were full of agony when he heard it. He didn't speak for a little bit then he said – and his voice was hoarse and whispery, "What can we do, Doctor? The disgrace will kill her mother." Dr. Harrison didn't say anything. He just went to a desk and opened it and took out a pretty yellow booklet with a gilt cupid on it and handed it to father. "Take this home and read it," he said. "It offers the best solution to the problem that I can devise." Father took the book like it was made of gold and put it carefully into his inside pocket and we came on home. All afternoon he and mother have been closet-

ed with that book and I have been left alone with my diary. I think mother must be a great deal better. I do wonder what is in the book.

Dec. 20 – At last I know what's in the yellow book! It tells about a place in Kansas City called "The Willows" where they take care of unfortunate girls like me. The babies are kept in a nursery and given the best care until homes are found for them. There are a great many homes where they want children and have none of their own. The Willows takes the babies of its patients and places them in these homes and has them adopted so they are just the same as if they were born in the home. I wonder if it can be possible I was selected by fate to bring a child into the world for some mother whose arms are aching for the baby she cannot have herself. I don't believe it, but it is hard to understand why things have to happen the way they do in this world. Why couldn't that mother have her own baby?

Dec. 21 – Dr. Harrison has written The Willows about the prices, which the yellow book says will be furnished upon application. It says they are reasonable and based on cost. I do hope it is not a cheap or low-class place. I never could stand it to go if it was. I have read the book through and through, and it leaves a good impression. It doesn't look cheap itself. While we are waiting to hear, mama says we will just go right along and make all our plans for Christmas as usual.

Feb. 10 – I am all ready to go to The Willows and I am really looking forward to the trip. Tomorrow we leave for Omaha. Mama is going with me and we are going to spend two weeks with Aunt Gene and then go on to Kansas City. Even Aunt Gene will not know where I am as she will think I am coming

MANSION ON A HILL

back home with mama and the people at home will think I am with Aunt Gene in Omaha. I think it is the dandiest scheme!

Today we came to The Willows.

Elizabeth goes on to describe her arrival in Kansas City and taxi ride to The Willows. She tells about the tour of the building and the nursery. She says there are blue ribbons on the boys' cribs and pink on the girls'. She loves that there is a piano in each lobby and the facility is lovely. Her mother is quite impressed with the facility and feels they made the right decision.

Feb 27 – The patients' rooms were nicely furnished. We were shown some that were not occupied. The one we selected for me is called the Princess Parlor. The name is on the door. It is furnished with white enamel furniture and is light and cheery. The woodwork through the whole hospital is white enameled, too, and is kept spotlessly clean, and the curtains and beds and everything are as white as snow.

After everything had been arranged, mama went on home on the evening train. I was brought back to my lobby and introduced to all the girls – just first names, of course, It seems awfully odd, but that is the rule here. No one knows anybody else's last name among the patients. Of course, I was dying with curiosity all the time about the girls, but I found them very much like any other bunch of girls that one might find anywhere. By supper time I began to feel somewhat at home among them.

When the supper bell rang, we all went down to the dining room – all except two girls who were in bed. There I saw the patients from the other parts of the hospital. We sat at long tables in the big dining room where everything is served just like it is at home. The lack of formality everywhere helps more than anything, I think, to put me at ease and make me forget I am away from home in a strange place. I was sure glad they had such a good supper as I was hungry as a wolf. I hope all the meals are always as good.

The diary continues, telling about Elizabeth's roommate Clara and other patients. Most are just like her – a student – but there is also a nurse, two school teachers, and a newspaper reporter. She shares how she plays the piano for the other girls. They rave about her playing. She also talks about the first examination day. She shares how nice and kind the doctor and nurses are to her.

MANSION ON A HILL

Laura played the piano in our lobby this evening.

March 3 – The doctor said I would be sick about July first. I think he is very competent. Everybody and everything here seem to give me more confidence as I learn more about them.

I wrote a long letter home today. I had wondered and wondered just how my correspondence could be handled as it would never do for mama or papa to write to me and address the letters here when I am supposed to be in Omaha. And I could not send letters to them from here in my own handwriting, either. At home everybody knows everybody's else's business and it would be all over town in a week just where I am and all our precautions would be in vain. But it is all very easy. My letters to them are all sent out with typewritten addresses and no one who handles them in the post-office at home can tell who they are from. My letters are sealed in enclosed envelopes addressed to the Superintendent instead of to me and I get them from the office after they have been delivered to him. Some of the girls who are known to be in Kansas City have their mail come to

KELLEE PARR

General Delivery and the postmaster forwards it to them here. There are several ways of solving the mail problems, they say.

Elizabeth shares about getting massages and how refreshing they are. They will help to keep her body from showing marks. (Quite different from Leona's opinion of the massages.) She talks about ordering out for ice cream and wafers one night, and the girls played charades. Sundays were very quiet days at The Willows, and she had feared they would be preached at there.

March 11 – We would make good subject matter for preachers and reformers – horrible examples, and all that sort of thing, but really, no one here ever takes that attitude. I am sure we are better for it, too, because as it is, we can keep our self-respect. When we get out in the world again, I know every girl here wants to show the Management that she can make good when given another chance, and that she will do her best to justify the faith placed in her. The right kind of treatment is worth more to us just now than any moral lectures could be. I am glad they realize this here and do not preach reform to us. We have all had our lesson good and plenty!

March 29 – Clara left today and it seems so funny to be in the room alone tonight. I am afraid I am the least bit homesick without her. We had a fruit feast tonight and everybody had to do a stunt. I sang "The Wild Man of Borneo" and Katy wiggled her ears and Madge played the piano with her back to it and the others did things just as foolish. We were just having a high old time when bedtime came and we had to hustle to get in by ten o'clock.

The rest of her diary tells of events that went on at The Willows. She got a new roommate after Clara became "sick" and went home.

Elizabeth's mother came to visit for a couple days. The girls also had a minstrel show, and Elizabeth laughed so hard she didn't feel right after. She became "sick" and had her baby on June 26. She named her baby girl Daphne, and she was beautiful.

> *July 10 – I am going home in the morning and I can hardly wait till I can see papa and mama again. Daphne was taken away today. I signed all the papers yesterday and she has been adopted by a professor and his wife in a great university. They came many miles for her and tonight I guess she is on the train with them speeding to her new home. I am glad and so thankful!*

Daphne was taken away today.

The last entry is dated August 1. Elizabeth has made it back home, and everything is different now. She doesn't see how she can fit back into her old life. She feels she has outgrown it.

> *August 1– I see that life is a serious matter and not play and I want to make the rest of my life count for something in the world. We have talked it over – papa, mama, and I – and we*

have decided that I shall go, the first of September, to Boston and study music. My music teacher says I have exceptional talent. I don't know that I have, but I think it would be wonderful to study just music. Papa has a sister there and I shall live with her while I am in Boston. Papa says she will look after me. But O, I wish I could make him understand – I'll never need any more looking after. I am not looking for a good time. All I want is a chance to work and be useful in the world and never to be a burden to him or mama.

The second document written by Mr. Haworth and copyrighted in 1918 is titled "By-Paths and Cross-Roads: Accidents of Fair Travelers on the Highway of Life." It begins with five fictitious stories dealing with quite different scenarios of young women who utilize the services of The Willows. This document shows Mr. Haworth's strong feelings against abortion. It emphasizes his desire to help the young woman to preserve the life of her unborn child, while being able to save her reputation.

1918 Document "By-Paths and Cross-Roads"[11]

The first is called "Sybil's Dilemma" and is the story of a young woman who finds herself pregnant, and her boyfriend has left to work in Brazil for a year. They had talked about marriage before he left but decided to wait until he got home, not knowing she was already pregnant. She cannot have a baby out of wedlock. Upon consulting her doctor, she has considered abortion, but he suggests The Willows as her solution. She agrees and is happy that her baby is adopted by a loving family. Months later after returning home she goes to see the doctor. She says, "Without an 'if' or a 'but,' I feel I have done my duty, not shirked it. I have given a new life to the world, not stifled one in the making. And while I did wrong in the first place, no one happily, knows it. And the experience is going to be worth the years of my life to me and make a woman of me. I can only say 'God bless you, doctor,' for sending me to that hospital."

"The Prima Donna's Decision" is the second story. It is the tale of a wealthy young woman named Bertha who is world renowned for her beautiful singing voice. She finds herself pregnant for a second time after a relationship that goes south. The first time she resolves the problem with an abortion. This time she contacts a new doctor for help. He is very kind and understanding, but he refuses to provide the service she desires. He instead encourages her to not destroy a life but to go to a maternity hospital in Kansas City and give birth to a child some other family would want to raise as their own. He assures her no one will know. Her reputation will be kept intact. The singer agrees it is the best solution and goes to The Willows.

After giving birth, her motherly instincts kick in, and she decides she cannot give up her baby. She chooses to keep him instead of placing him for adoption. She has fame and fortune. She can survive any scrutiny society places on her. Another girl in seclusion too decides she wants to keep her baby, but Bertha convinces her to give the baby up for adoption because she did not have the means to make it in the harsh world as a single mother with a child. Three years later Bertha has continued her wonderful career and raised her child. She begins taking part in the filming of a play for the moving-picture screen. In the process her three-year-old baby is discovered and stars with his mother in the film. He becomes an overnight sensation. She runs into the doctor who saved her son's life and says, "Doctor, I thank both God and you every day for my son. Truly, I shudder sometimes at the very thought that I came so near not having him at all. Oh, how I adore him!"

The third story is titled "A Cancer Case" and is about an older married woman who asks her doctor to operate on her because she is certain she has cancer and is dying, as did many others in her family who were so inflicted. She had lost an infant child as well. The wise doctor upon examining her realized she was a hypochondriac and did not have cancer. She was quite healthy, but what she sorely missed in her life was a child to raise. He suggests to the woman's husband they adopt a baby. The doctor gave him the information about The Willows and the fine babies they had available for adoption. The story ends with the couple happy with their newly adopted baby. The doctor asks the new mother about her cancer. The woman replies, "Bless you doctor. I don't know just what it was you gave me, but it certainly cured me. I haven't felt it since the day I asked you to operate on me."

The next story is called "Dr. Kellum's Last Abortion." Dr. Kellum is a doctor who is a well-respected doctor in an upper-class neighborhood. Unbeknownst to many, he has performed private abortions for many of the high society women. A single socialite comes to him who has had an affair with a married man and ask for him to perform the procedure. The man will surely pay any price. The doctor agrees on a price of $500 and sets an appointment for later in the week. The next day the doctor receives word his college-age daughter is deathly ill, and he rushes to her bedside. He discovers she had relations with a young man over the summer, and – without talking to her father – she had an abortion. Something went wrong and the girl's dying words to her father were to ask him to promise to never do what her doctor had done to her. He promised to never perform such an operation on another young woman. Later in the week when he meets the young woman in trouble, he tells her of his daughter, explaining why he cannot perform the abortion. He has another solution for her. He tells her about a maternity hospital in Kansas City. He is sure the married man would be able to cover the expenses. The girl agrees and says, "Yes, doctor I will. What you tell me is a terrible story, but it makes me see things in a different light. Your daughter was right in her dying request. I am glad to be your last abortion patient."

"Margaret's New Profession" is the final story and is about a woman whose younger sister Ethel discovers her fiancé to have drowned in a horrific accident. Ethel was to be married in just weeks. She finds out she is four months pregnant and doesn't know what to do. Margaret consults a doctor who provides information about a maternity hospital and nobody would have to know of Ethel's condition. Ethel goes to The Willows. In her letters home to Margaret, she shares how wonderful the staff is and how she thinks Margaret would herself make a wonderful nurse. A couple years after Ethel's return, Margaret finds herself unemployed after her employers' bankruptcy. Not knowing what to do, her sister's letter came to mind about her making a good nurse. Margaret looked at the catalog from previous years from The Willows about their school for nurses. It was a fourteen-month course. She applied and was accepted. Upon completion of her course work, Margaret said to Ethel, "Do you know I am so happy in this work and that I sometimes thank Providence that you had to be sent to the hospital. That may not sound very nice, dear, but when you consider the happy outcome of that trouble both for yourself and for me, I think you will agree with me that even the dark chapter has had a happy ending."

In the rest of this document, Mr. Haworth goes on to explain their mission at The Willows.

> *The Willows Maternity Sanitarium is an institution devoted exclusively to the care and seclusion of unfortunate young women, offering them congenial, homelike surroundings before confinement and exceptional medical and hospital care during delivery and convalescence. In most cases arrangements are also made for the finding of a home for the patient's baby for adoption.*

All of the advertisements for The Willows spoke of the quality of care provided for the residents. However, in the earlier years of operation, there is documentation not all Kansas Citians believed The Willows and other maternity hospitals were good environments for these young women. They also complained the facilities were costing the city money. In an article from *The Kansas City Times* dated April 9, 1913, the superintendent of the General Hospital filed a complaint to the Missouri State Health Board about the lack of sanitary condition and lack of staff at facilities, specifically naming the Willows Maternity Sanitarium and the Fairmount Maternity Sanitarium. He also stated that advertising to bring girls to these facilities resulted in at least twenty-

MANSION ON A HILL

five young women being sent to the General Hospital once their funds were exhausted. They became city charges, and it cost General Hospital $1000 that year to provide care for them and their babies.

After an investigation with reports given to the overseeing health board committee, the recommendations were made that a resident physician of undoubted standing should be employed on a salary and have no other financial connections to the sanitarium. A high-class nurse should be in charge of training schools for employees. A pathologist from the General Hospital would do regular checkups on the sterility of the delivery room. Finally, the board recommended that more care should be exercised in allowing babies to be adopted from these sanitariums. The health board allowed the facilities to remain open, and these new regulations only aided in providing better conditions for the girls.

The Willows Maternity Sanitarium
A STRICTLY ETHICAL HOME AND HOSPITAL FOR
THE CARE OF SECLUSION MATERNITY PATIENTS

1911 Futuristic Drawing of The Willows with the Annex Added
Drawing courtesy of Carol Haworth Price

Chapter 5

The "Ritz"

Both the capacity and reputation of The Willows grew over its years of operation. Those in the adoption field referred to The Willows as the "Ritz" or the "Waldorf" of the Kansas City facilities. It was one of the largest and longest operating of all the maternity homes. The Willows was known as a highly respectable establishment and reported that only finest young women were allowed to stay there.

The Haworth family would not accept federal aid, grants, donations, or any other moneys with strings attached. They wanted complete autonomy in being able to take in the types of girls they wanted with no obligation to anyone. Mr. Haworth wrote a thirty-two-page document in 1927 used for advertising to doctors called "Who Will Help – How to Get Help." [12]

```
                WHO
              Will Help
              ▼ ▼ ▼ ▼
                HOW
              To Get Help
```

1927 Brochure "Who Will Help – How to Get Help"
Mr. Haworth shares the philosophy of why they did not accept outside resources. He wrote:

> *The Willows has back of its operating expense no church, philanthropic organization, foundation or endowment fund. We have intentionally refrained from seeking charity support as such in order that we should not be forced to take into our institution nor even feel that we were under any obligation to take into it, patients that we would not wish to have associated with our higher grade unfortunate girls. In this way we are able to control the standard of morals in the place, keeping a high social atmosphere among our patients.*

They had hundreds of applications for each bed. Only those who could afford to pay the fees for services were approved, taking into consideration morals and attitude of the potential patient. Prior to the home's closing, Garnet Haworth was quoted in a July 15, 1969 article from *The Kansas City Star* newspaper saying, "To my knowledge, this is the first privately-owned hospital of its kind to come into existence and probably the only one functioning in the U.S. today."[13]

All of the services provided by The Willows came at a healthy price. The fees charged were too expensive for many families. In the 1920s the stay for a girl was said to be costlier than the most expensive finishing schools. The Willows' girls often came from upper-class families and were well educated. Girls with fewer financial resources shared less expensive rooms or stayed in the annexed cottages. They were allowed to do household duties to help defray the cost of room and board.

Mr. Haworth did not mince words when sharing how expensive it was for young ladies to stay at The Willows. He did not want others to see their facility as a charity. It was there to provide a service to girls from reputable families who the Haworths felt would be chastised in society because of their circumstances. The Willows provided a secluded, clean environment for the babies to be born safely and where the girls' reputations could be saved. The 1927 document "Who Will Help – How to Get Help" also enlightens one to Mr. Haworth's business mindset and how he and Mrs. Haworth kept their facility in operation. Suggestions were given to girls and their families on how to get the money to pay for their stay at The Willows. Particular care is noted not to damage the girl's reputation by sharing the situation with too many people. It could be calamitous for the girl, the boy, their families and even the community. A section titled "Suggested Ways to Get Money" states:

> *Parents do not always have the means to help their daughters. Sometimes the father is living on a small salary and has to*

> *depend on some payment plan. Or being a farmer, he may have growing grain for livestock that are not immediately cashable. Banks, business friends or other relatives can often be resorted to. The Hospital has in extreme cases taken real estate mortgages, chattel mortgages and even bankable notes. However, where bankable notes are given, patrons usually prefer going directly to their own bank and procuring the money and have the Hospital or its Management in no way involved in the matter.*

The article goes on to suggest if a girl's parents need financial help, the girl may want to confide in a friend, talk to the pastor or elders in a church tolerant to youth, get help from a sister or brother, or check with uncles, aunts or a favorite cousin. Also noted is that sometimes a girl might know a man who loves her but who is not responsible for her condition. He might be willing to finance her confinement and afterward marry her. One paragraph titled "Better Ask Help Than Be Ruined" encourages:

> *So the patient and those interested in her, when sufficient funds for the grade of services she should have are otherwise unavailable, should not hesitate to offer the opportunity of assisting in financing her to those who have a personal or friendly interest in her and the family. And in this connection, it is not advisable that a girl try to skimp herself by being satisfied with a grade of services below those that harmonize with her education and rearing. Particularly is this true when it involves services that might leave her condition subject to discovery after she had returned home and the case apparently over.*

Leona never knew just how much Mr. Belt shelled out to cover up his son's irresponsible behavior, but she was indeed fortunate he chose The Willows. It is difficult to find documentation of just what the charges were for a girl's stay at The Willows. One document sheds some light at what the cost might have been around the time Leona was there in 1924 to 1925. It is called "The Basis of Estimating the Charges for the Care of a Patient at The Willows Sanitarium."

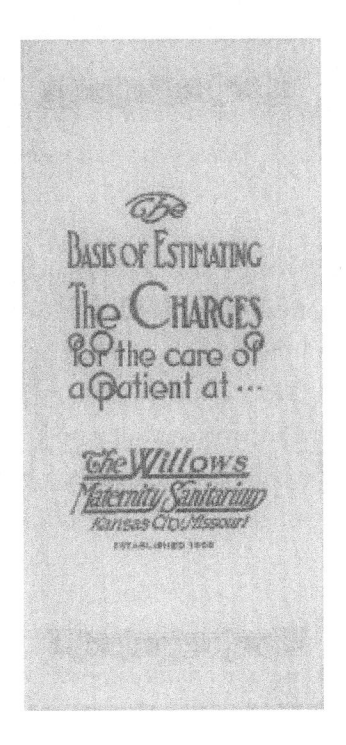

1920's Brochure "Basis of Estimating the Charges for the Care of a Patient at The Willows Maternity Sanitarium"[14]

The brochure begins by stating that the girls should enter the facility as early as possible.

> Patients may enter as early before confinement as they desire. They frequently enter three, four, five and six months in advance of accouchement, in which case the charge for the time previous to the date of expectancy is estimated merely at the room, board and laundry rate for the room occupied. Patients

are safer here and can be better cared for than is possible at home. As a matter of fact, they should enter when they are about half way in the duration of pregnancy. This permits them to get away from home before suspicion of their condition is aroused through changed physical form. True, the occasional patient may show her condition earlier through facial features, liver spots and the like. Of course, the most dangerous of early symptoms is perhaps "morning sickness." In cases of these kinds, action should be taken accordingly to meet the need of the expectant mother.

But never should a patient enter after the seventh month. Not only on account of the increase in abdominal size but due to changes to adjustment that nature makes at that time. The patient should be in the Sanitarium, her mental worries over and her nerves adjusted before her period comes upon here.

The brochure goes into great detail explaining the quality of care provided. It breaks down the cost for the different living areas and the cost for each service provided.

Charges for Room and Board: (with two individual beds in a room and includes board, laundry, and general care for the duration of stay in the hospital)

Main Building Room and Board: **$22.00 to $26.00 per week**

North Wing Room and Board: (First floor Sanitarium North Wing-similar to Main Building but less elaborate) **$12.00 to $19.00 per week**

Cottages: (two buildings connected with Main Building by area-ways) Less expensive accommodations for those who find lobby space in the Main Building beyond their means) **No price shown.**

Mr. Haworth explained the cost during confinement:

The Convalescent Department is provided for the care of the patients following confinement. No extra charge is made for hospitalization during this period, and the three weeks allowed for convalescence are figured on the same basis as that of the room selected by the patient when she enters. Thus, the patient is assured home life prior to delivery and hospital services following delivery, room and board at no more than the rates charged her during her waiting period.

Charges for Medical Services: (if covered by House Obstetrician) **$50.00 and upward** Patients may have their own physician and charges omitted.

Charges of High-Grade General Nursing: (provided for three weeks following confinement for recovery) **$35.00**

Charges for Confinement: (use of delivery room, extra nursing attention, stock drugs used, and special laundry of bed and linens) **$15.00**

Charges for Laboratory Fees: (includes routine Wassermann test, and urinalysis) **$10.00**

Charge for Normal Healthy Child: (for keeping child until home is found) **$30.00**

It was almost impossible to determine a fair prior cost for the care of an infant. Mr. Haworth gave an explanation in the brochure about the $30.00 fee and how this is really a nominal charge for the services provided.

Then the care of the child in the Nursery, keeping it until a home is found for it, and finding a home, means a service out of proportion to anything, results considered, ever attempted and attained in this country.

As there is no sanitarium of similar size and services in the United States making a specialty of caring for and protecting unmarried girls and young women, and finding homes for their babies when desired, there is little opportunity for comparing expense rates, when one considers that the babies are an expensive part of the work, costing approximately $10.00 per week to be cared for when well and requiring $15.00 to $20.00 a week services when sick – with some babies requiring six weeks, two to three months or longer, their expense seems to be very reasonable.

There is no way the Nursery can be made self-supporting from receipts that are collected directly for it. The legitimate fee that might more properly be made for taking care of the average child that is left for adoption is $100.00, instead of the nominal fee that is now charged.

A girl's family only paid the one-time $30.00 fee no matter how long the baby resided at the Willows. The adoptive parents also were not charged for the care of the infant. The infant was The Willow's financial responsibility beyond the $30.00 child care charge they received. It was imperative for profitability to have the babies healthy and adopted as quickly as possible.

Using these prices, an estimate of the cost for Leona's stay at The Willows can be calculated. She entered on November 17, 1924 and delivered on February 14, 1925. If she remained the average of three weeks after delivery, she would have stayed between fifteen and sixteen weeks.

For estimation purposes, let's assume Leona stayed in the Main Building at $22.00 per week for sixteen weeks. The costs for her stay would be:

Room and board: 16 weeks at $22 per week.	$352.00
Nursing care:	$35.00
Confinement fee:	$15.00
Laboratory fee:	$10.00
Healthy Child fee:	$30.00
Total	$442.00

Mr. Belt's $442.00 bill would equate to $6,298.47 in 2018. In the 1950s through the 1960s, it is rumored to have set back a girl's family between $5,000 and $10,000 for a three or four month "visit."

Many have questioned whether The Willows made money from the adoption of the infants or if they sold babies. The maternity hospital strictly made their profit from the caring of the pregnant girls. They did not make money off of the adoption of the infants as this would have appeared to be trafficking the babies. The cost to the adoptive parents was limited to the court fees and processing of the adoption, which was handled strictly through the Missouri courts.

The Willows staff always strived to find superior, God-fearing couples for their babies. They promised the biological mothers that their babies would be placed with good families. An article from the *Lawrence Journal-World* from June 21, 1975 described The Willows in the 1920s. It describes the strict guidelines for admittance of girls and selection of adoptive families. It stated:

> *This was the racy, roaring '20s in wild, rich Kansas City. The Willows was like the Ritz or the Waldorf of homes for unwed*

mothers. It had a lot of snob appeal and the owners were members of Kansas City society.

The original owners were Edwin and Cora May Haworth, in conjunction with Dr. John W. Kepner. Operation of The Willows was very strict. Not just every unwed mother could get in. They were recommended by prominent doctors throughout the United States, and not everyone qualified to adopt the babies. Some prominent entertainers were refused simply because they were in that ugly, dirty entertainment business.[15]

The girls' families were told when they entered if a baby could not be found an adoptive home in a reasonable amount of time, her family was responsible to come back and take the baby home. Returning a child would not have been good for business. The Willows advertised extensively in the 1910s and 1920s, placing ads in newspapers stating they had babies for adoption. It was imperative to find homes for the babies to be able to have room for additional unwed girls. Surprisingly, the advertisements were mostly about boys, as the nursery was often full of baby boys. There was a larger demand for blue-eyed baby girls. Because of their high society clientele, the Haworth's advertised having "Bright babies with exceptional parentage of above average health and intelligence." Some of the ads that ran in *The Kansas City Star* newspaper included:

> **September 6, 1918** *"SAVE THAT BABY—AMERICA NEEDS IT" 20 choice boys and girls ranging in age up to 10 months. Call personally or write The Willows 2929 Main St.*

> **December 1, 1919** *FOR ADOPTION—20 bright, intelligent healthy boys, ranging in age up to 9 months, will furnish description of parentage to those making an application. Write or call personally. The Willows 2929 Main St.*

November 25, 1922 *DO YOU REALIZE what a boy means to your family circle? "Sonny" for short and "Sunny" for the brightness he brings. Many bright, attractive, healthy boy babies for adoption, ranging in age up to 12 months. Call or write for booklet and information. The Willows 2929 Main St.*

December 10, 1925 *A MERRY CHRISTMAS—Why not brighten your home this Christmas by adopting an attractive, healthy boy? We have 30 boys of exceptional parentage ranging in age up to 6 months. For further information write or call personally. The Willows 2929 Main Street*

At the end of 1925, the year Leona was at The Willows, the Haworth's and others with homes for unwed women ran into a small issue with the Children's Bureau of the State Board of Health. The board passed a rule that the homes in Kansas City could no longer advertise having babies for adoption. When Mr. Haworth failed to appear at a meeting about his not getting a permit from the board, they ordered no more patients could be received at The Willows until the permit was obtained. The permit was received, but this ruling seemed to curtail the extensive advertising Mr. Haworth had utilized to get the word out that babies were available for adoption.

Mr. Haworth came up with another brilliant advertising idea once the board banned the newspaper ads. In the 1930s, The Willows created a couple of new documents that showed happy, beautiful babies who had been adopted by families. They were a testimony to the quality of babies they placed in private homes. The first document was called the "Album of Willows Babies." Couples who inquired about adopting would be sent a copy of this document to peruse. It filled the inquiring couple with the hope and excitement of adopting their own child.

A second document was written in 1930 by Mrs. E. P. Haworth titled "Baby Bares." She showed her writing skills matched her husband's. This booklet was directed at married women with no children and considering adoption. The introduction in the booklet states, "This booklet is devoted to study of mother-psychology and mother-instincts and consideration of feelings and sentiments that are beyond the understanding of a man, except in a superficial and objective way."[16]

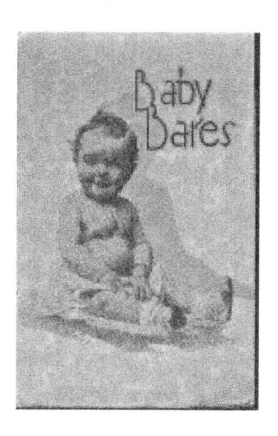

1930 Document "Baby Bares"

Mrs. Haworth begins her twenty-four-page booklet by talking about children's love for baby bears, especially Teddy Bears named for Teddy Roosevelt. She equates the joy children have for their Teddy Bears to the joy of motherhood and bundles of "baby bares," amusingly using the homonym. She writes passionately about the bond between "baby bares" and mothers. Something, according to Mrs. Haworth, men do not understand. Her whole point is to emphasize the importance of adoption for the "poor woman who has no child, who can have no child of her own. She writes:

> *What greater punishment is conceivable to the woman of normal instincts than the denial to her motherhood? What is the answer to this problem? Is there an answer?*
>
> *Yes, there is an answer. The adoption of the offspring of the higher grade unfortunate girl is the answer that has proven efficacious for the thousands. But what of these few thousands*

KELLEE PARR

for the quarter century The Willows has been serving childless homes!

Mrs. Haworth shares in her booklet the importance of the work of The Willows providing high-grade children. She goes into great detail explaining the difference of their work from other homes and the quality of the babies they have for adoption. Photos of beautiful "baby bares" are shown throughout the booklet.

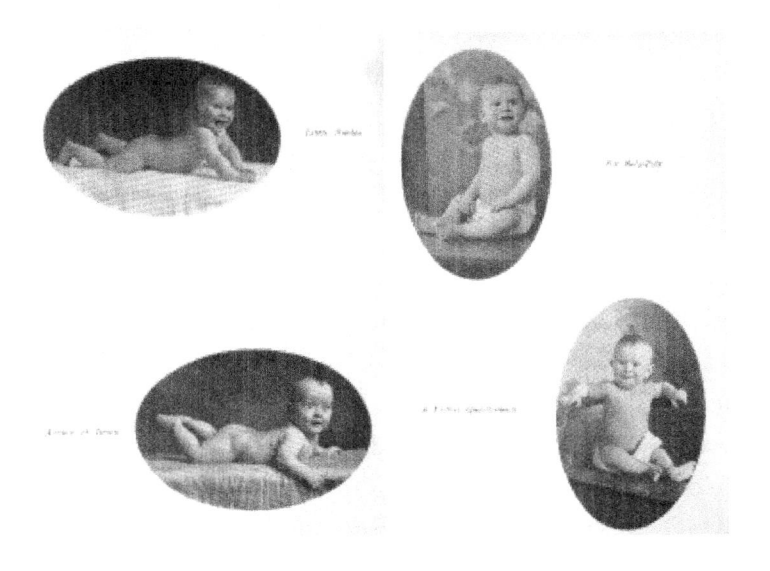

1930 Document "Baby Bares"

Over the years, there was a huge demand for The Willows babies as well as from the other Kansas City facilities for unwed mothers, especially around the holidays. This article from *The Kansas City Star* expresses the huge request for babies in 1934:

December 16, 1934
Kansas City Star
Kansas City, Missouri
YULE GIFTS TO CUDDLE

MANSION ON A HILL

REQUESTS FOR BABIES TO ADOPT EXCEED THE SUPPLY HERE

As Christmas Approaches, Childless Homes Open Their Doors to Take in Permanently the Little Ones.

More babies are sought for permanent adoption in Kansas City this Christmas season than can be supplied by the two principal sources, The Willows and the Fairmount maternity homes.

A baby a day, on an average, has been let for adoption by the Willows in the last six weeks, and the Fairmount home could have met that average if it had had enough babies. As it is, the Fairmount has been providing about twenty babies a month for adoption.

As Christmas approaches, the demand for babies increases from childless parents. Some of them have been waiting for the right sort of baby for months.

"I have the tree, the lights, and the gifts," one woman told Mrs. H. S. Lane, superintendent of the Fairmount. "All I need now is the baby.".

"So strong is the demand for squirming, kicking little Christmas gifts that the babies are seldom more than 2 weeks old before they are adopted at this time of year," Mrs. Lane added. "Two-at-a-time adoptions are increasing in popularity, perhaps because of a growing notion that companionship will be an asset in such an upbringing. Only last week a Kansas City woman adopted two 2-week-old infants," Mrs. Lane said.

"A child in the home at Christmas seems to complete the picture." Mrs. Lane concluded.[17]

In 1925, the adoptive parents of Leona's baby sent a request to The Willows to adopt a baby girl. They had already adopted a boy in 1920 from the home. They received a letter from Mrs. Nellie McEwen, The Willows secretary, dated March 21, 1925. It stated they had a baby girl available if the couple could get to Kansas City on Tuesday, March 24 or Wednesday, March 25. The mother and baby had both been tested for any social diseases, using the Wasserman blood test. Both tests were negative. There was a $10 fee for the tests, along with the adoption court processing fee of $21, for a total of $31 to be paid by the adoptive parents. The letter stated that if they arrived early enough in the morning, all arrangements could be made and completed so the couple and baby could return home the evening of the same day.

The letter also provided details about feeding the baby. The Willows fed their babies cow's milk. They gave a formula for preparing the infant's food. They suggested the couple bring a quart Thermos bottle and two Hygeia nursing bottles, or they could obtain them from The Willows upon their arrival. The letter stated the facility would provide sufficient food for the return trip home.

Chapter 6

The Mission

The Haworth family was devoted to providing a very needed and confidential service to families all across America. It was their mission to help these desperate, disparaged girls and their families to cover up the girls' sexual indiscretions or to hide pregnancies of victims of sexual abuse. They wanted to save the reputation of these girls and make embarrassing situations discreetly go away. The Willows provided anonymity and protection. "They were given a name when they came in they went by and that way it was kept a total secret," Carol Haworth Price said. "It was so awful for them. I can't even imagine that people were that uncaring, unkind, and hurtful. These girls were not bad girls. As we all know these things happen and they still happen today."

After the girls' three, four or even up to eight months' stay in seclusion, the babies were delivered and the young mothers returned home empty handed to carry the burden of their secrets for the rest of their lives. The babies were found new homes, while their biological mothers hoped their children were provided much better lives than they could have given them.

In the introduction of The Willows' 1927 document "Who Will Help – How to Get Help," Mr. Haworth shares the struggle he felt in handling the truth of the situation in which the girls had found themselves. He states:

> *We do not know whether we will ever be forgiven for the misrepresentations our business forces us to make or not. These misrepresentations are what some would call white lies. Whether a white lie is ever white or not or whether it is purely a lie is questioned by some people. But if we are going to save an unfortunate girl from the social and possibly moral degradation that would come with public knowledge of her misfortune, the white lie must often be involved.*

The document goes on to offer suggestions to help the girls figure out what "little white lies" they might use or not use to hide their circumstances. He did emphasize first the importance of being as forthright and honest as possible, especially with their immediate families. However, young women were encouraged to be careful who they did share information with so their privacy would be assured. Mr. Haworth continued:

> *Our American citizenship being generally frank and honest people, they never like to tell an untruth. And the closer they can stick to actual facts with safety, the better satisfied they usually feel. For the very reason that it is so close to the facts of the case it becomes suggestive of the actual facts.*

> *Let it be understood that these methods suggested here are not made for the purpose of encouraging unfortunate young women in deception or misrepresentation, particularly to their own people. We do not favor misrepresentation to the family, although it is often not necessary and also inadvisable to take all members of the family into one's confidence. But we believe that there is almost never a family in which someone should not be entrusted with the confidence of the girl.*

MANSION ON A HILL

He goes into quite detail explaining the pros and cons of each excuse that might be given. Some of these "little white lies" found in the brochure for girls to ponder include:

- *Leaving School for Sickness – so it often saves the reputation of the girl and her family when no other excuse would suffice and without arousing suspicion, plus provides the need for funds.*

- *Climatic Change for Medical Reasons – sometimes a prolonged rest with a change of climate is advised by the doctor on the case. Often a family member travels with the patient to help her to get her satisfactorily located and her supposed treatment or medical service arranged for, to return two or three days later, supposedly having accompanied the patient to her destination.*

- *Surgical Operation Excuse – A surgical operation, particularly one for a tumor, is a possible excuse though rarely safe as it might necessitate in the extreme case the showing of an abdominal scar evidencing the supposed operation, to some members of the immediate family or even to girlfriends, if she be athletically inclined or intimately associated with other girls.*

- *Kinds of School to Be Attended – an excuse that is very practical and frequently used for both obtaining money and as a reason for being away from home is school work. It is not always best to be too specific as to what school one is at in case there is any likelihood of someone writing or visiting a young woman. Sometimes it is necessary to well oil the wheels of the postal service in order that no later friction arise and burn out a bearing. With the postal service well planned, the patient may apparently be in some other school or town during the whole time she is at The Willows.*

- *Educational Work Good Excuse – particularly is educational work resorted to excuse girls from home and associates if they are of satisfactory school age for the particular kind of school they choose. Especially is this desirable at seasons of the year when school changes are common. School work is particularly a good excuse for calling in financial assistance.*

- *Nursing Dangerous Excuse – a word of caution is possibly advisable regarding using a training school as an excuse for leaving home. The preliminary requirements for being admitted to any high-grade training school to establish the social and moral standing of the prospective pupil are so specific and exacting that it is hardly safe to attempt to enter a training school. Especially is it dangerous for a patient to claim she is entering training at The Willows (nursing school). The Willows' standards and requirements are more fully advertised to the doctors in the two score surrounding states to which its literature goes than probably any other training school in the territory. So, it is so simple to check up on her if she be in The Willows' Training School that this is one plan particularly to be avoided.*

- *Commercial School – a plan that has worked quite successfully among patients has been the excuse of taking a commercial course. Patients rent typewriters and can, even with the retarding energy due to their late period of gestation, accomplish quite a little in preparing themselves for typist work.*

- *Visiting Relatives as an Excuse – many young women are sent away on visits. (As in Leona's case, to go and help her sister take care of her children.) These may be in connection with a nervous or physical near- or complete-breakdown, or it may be just for the change.*

MANSION ON A HILL

- *Workers Change Location – it is quite frequent that patients who are old enough to take up some line of work and earn their own living or who have been doing so, may make the excuse that they want to change and come to Kansas City, or apparently to some other place, and thus find a satisfactory excuse for being away from home, friends, and associates.*

- *Plans May Change Before Returning Home – it is to be kept in mind that people can always change their minds. They may stay at a job for two or three months or even six months and decide they are not adapted to it or do not like it. Then they may go back to their old lines of work, their old job and nothing be thought of it.*

- *Handicap of Occupational Excuse – the one difficulty that has to be allowed for when a move for a change of occupation is made is that it lacks the excuse for procuring funds for expenses. For surely if a young woman is working she can make enough to live on.*

Many girls and families struggled with how to keep this situation a secret. Whether the excuse given was to be visiting family, having an illness, starting a new job, or moving to new part of the country, each girl struggled with a situation that would alter her life forever. The Willows' goal was to protect each girl from the harsh judgment of society, however they could not erase the event or the loss of a child from the girl's memory.

Chapter 7

Early Years by the Numbers

Being a prolific author, Mr. Haworth in 1925 created a twenty-five-page brochure specifically pointing out numbers and data about the girls at The Willows in the year 1920. It was titled "Who Enter Here Find Quiet and Peace and Rest" and sent to thousands of doctors in nearby states.

1925 brochure "Who Enter Here Find Quiet and Peace and Rest" The brochure was filled with photos of Willows babies placed in adoptive homes. It showed the staff members and highlighted rooms in the facility. Doctors were invited to contact The Willows to receive even more detailed information in a ninety-page catalogue and to ask for rates. "Who Enter Here" shared that three hundred forty-three girls from twenty-nine different states had babies at The Willows in 1920.

MANSION ON A HILL

THE WILLOWS ALMOST COVERS THE ENTIRE COUNTRY.

The shaded states represent the twenty-nine states from which girls came to The Willows in 1920.

After The Willows had been in operation for nearly a quarter century, Mr. Haworth created the document "A Ten Years' Survey of Seclusion Maternity Service: A Sociological Analysis of the Patients Cared for by The Willows Maternity Sanitarium Covering the Ten-year Period, 1920–1929 Inclusive." This survey provides illuminating information about the ages, residency, education levels, occupations, religions, and numbers of patients at The Willows over the ten-year period from 1920 until 1929. The data would have included Leona's information. The number of girls that passed through The Willows' door ranged from 258 to 344 girls per year. A total of 3,021 girls were patients, representing forty-one states, the territory of Hawaii, and Canada. This document was made available to doctors throughout the country. It strived to show the quality of girls and the history of The Willows. It presented a good case for a solution that doctors could share with their patients. The introductory page read:

It is very difficult to tell or show other people just what class of unfortunate young women are cared for at The Willows Maternity Sanitarium. And erroneous ideas of patients and the work done for them is often held by the uninitiate.

Pause, Doctor, you who may never have sent a patient for Willows' services, and who on first thought may be inclined to charge that the world is going to the dogs – pause, we say, and reflect that these patients are drawn from one hundred twenty-three million people and over a period of ten years' time. Then you will realize that all the high-grade girls are not necessarily going to the bad. But on the other hand, you will recognize that few are they who these days are free from and above temptation!

After perusing this review, the doctor will not hesitate in recommending any good girl who has made the error of the flesh, to repair to The Willows for seclusion and protection. Any fear he or the patient's family might have of her being thrown among undesirable patients and under demoralizing influences, will be dispelled by the charts herein presented.

Never elsewhere has so remarkable a group of unfortunates been assembled into a single institution for seclusion maternity services.

Truly these are the ACCIDENTS OF SOCIETY.

The patients at The Willows during this ten-year period ranged in age from twelve to over twenty-six. It is hard to believe that girls as young as twelve needed the assistance The Willows provided. This is the chart showing the ages of the 3,021 girls there from 1920 until 1929.

MANSION ON A HILL

Age				
• Twelve	2	• Twenty	358
• Thirteen	16	• Twenty-one	249
• Fourteen	36	• Twenty-two	217
• Fifteen	91	• Twenty-three	163
• Sixteen	177	• Twenty-four	112
• Seventeen	320	• Twenty-five	105
• Eighteen	377	• Twenty-six	77
• Nineteen	416	• Unknown	34
		Total	3,021

In 1925, the year Leona was there, girls came from twenty-one different states. The distribution of states and numbers for each was as follows:

States			
• Missouri	60	• Indiana	16
• Iowa	51	• Arkansas	8
• Kansas	48	• Colorado	8
• Illinois	41	• South Dakota	8
• Nebraska	26	• North Dakota	5
• Oklahoma	25	• Mississippi	2
• Minnesota	17	• New Mexico	2
• Kentucky, Ohio, Pennsylvania, West Virginia, Wyoming			1 each
		Total	344

More girls from the nearby states were sent to The Willows in the beginning of its operation. By 1969, every state in the union was represented as well as many foreign countries. In the earlier years, almost all the girls arrived by train. The distribution among states started to spread as better transportation modes became available. In the 1960s, Garnet Haworth, owner and superintendent of The Willows, would personally go to the Kansas City airport to meet girls arriving by plane.

The girls that came to The Willows in the early days were mostly country girls with upbringing similar to Leona's. Approximately 90% of The Willows' patients were from rural and small communities. If the survey had been taken in the 50s and 60s, it is quite possible the results would have been reversed. The community environment makeup of the 344 girls from 1925 was:

Community Environment	
• Country	155
• Town	117
• Country and Town	37
• City	35

Another interesting feature from the survey was the educational level of the girls. The range is from common school (up through eighth grade) through college graduate. Leona was in the common school group as she only finished eighth grade.

Education			
• Common School	89	• One Year College	15
• One Year High	34	• Two Years College	13
• Two Years High	39	• Three Years College	6
• Three Years High	48	• College Graduate	9
• High School Graduate	91		

Occupation was another facet shared in the survey. In the 1920s, 54% of the girls were students or home girls who were completely dependent on family for support. Of the 344 girls in 1925, 107 were students and 94 were listed as home girls. This was 58% of the girls. Leona would have been listed as one of the students. The remaining 143 girls held the following occupations:

Occupations			
• Teachers	32	• Beauty Operators	3
• Domestic or Waitresses	31	• Milliners	2
• Business College Trained	22	• Photographer	1
• Nurses	14	• Bank Cashier	1
• Sales	12	• Dressmaker	1
• Clerical or Office Workers	10	• Government Clerk	1
• Telephone Operators	9	• Interior Designer	1
• Factory Workers	3		

Religion was another area that was identified in the survey. The Willows was proud of the fact that 85% of the patients were church members and the remaining 15% were almost all church attendants with a church preference, though not actual members. Mr. Haworth wrote:

> *The fact that so large a proportion of the patients are church members, would indicate that they are not birth controlists and that the church has made them too conscientious to resort to birth control or abortion either as a means to sexual indulgence and lasciviousness. And that a young woman requires services from The Willows, does not show her to be immoral, but rather to have been a victim of circumstances or of weakness at most. But she has not lost her self-respect nor turned to immoral practices for her relaxation or for means of sustenance.*

Religion				
• Methodist	82	• Congregational	15
• Baptist	49	• Episcopal	5
• Catholic	39	• Evangelical	2
• Christian	33	• United Brethren	2
• Lutheran	32	• Church of Christ	2
• Presbyterian	22	• Friends	1

Mr. Haworth noted in this publication that he didn't see any significant reason for the fact that there were more than twice as many Methodists as any other denomination. He noted:

> *The preponderance of Methodists in the Central States from which so large a portion of our patients are derived accounts for this strong lead.*

However, in an earlier publication he noted that the allowance of dancing by Methodists "increased temptation that often led to promiscuity." Leona belonged to the Methodist Church in her little town so she was one of 82 Methodists at The Willows in 1925. Leona hid her best dress in the rafters of the outhouse and snuck out that night to go to a dance where she met "the most handsomest boy." Mr. Haworth would no doubt have found this telling.

Chapter 8

Life at The Willows
(1924)

As Leona entered this strange world, she was shocked at the grandeur of The Willows. She had never seen anything like it in her life. She was reminded of her favorite book *Alice in Wonderland*. She had read it at school and understood how Alice felt entering an unusual new land. As she and Nurse Reed made their way down the foyer to the admissions office, Leona stopped to look at her reflection in the large mirror on the ornate walnut and marble console. The mirror almost reached to the top of the ten-foot ceiling.

A music box that was three-feet long and played twelve songs sat on the credenza. Nurse Reed stopped, opened the lid and played the first song for Leona. For just a moment, Leona forgot her woes. She loved music. The beautiful song touched her heart. Nurse Reed explained the song was written by a famous Russian composer named Tchaikovsky and was titled "Waltz of the Flowers" from the ballet "The Nutcracker." Leona's knowledge of music and books would be expanded during her stay. Too quickly the song was over and the reality of the moment set in.

Nurse Reed showed Leona to the admissions office. Mrs. Maudene Lowe and Mrs. Nellie McEwen were there to greet her with some paperwork to sign, including documents that said Leona would relinquish all rights to her baby once it was born. In a daze after receiving an explanation of these important papers, Leona signed them.

Many of the staff members spent their entire careers at The Willows. They were dedicated to the Haworths' mission. Mrs. Lowe and Mrs. McEwen were just two such employees. Shortly after meeting Mrs. Lowe, Leona was taken to the Superintendent's office. She was introduced to Mrs. Cora Haworth, wife of owner E. P. Haworth. Though Mrs. Haworth was a no-nonsense kind of person, she was a very loving and helped Leona to feel welcome.

Cora May Haworth in her office in 1920
Photo courtesy of Carol Haworth Price

Leona was shown her bedroom and the rest of her new home where she would be living the next few months. The Willows included a large library and parlor where she and the other girls could pass their time reading, playing innocent games of amusement, or just holding pleasant conversation. Those who played the piano or another instrument would entertain the other girls, who would often sing along. Mrs. Haworth strived to provide culture and knowledge to the young ladies. They were taught to sew, embroider, knit and crochet to pass the time away.

MANSION ON A HILL

All the girls were encouraged to take advantage of the large library. Workers brought magazines from home to stock the library with popular reading material of the day. Management was quite proud of the extensive library of light and modern fiction because as noted in one of Mr. Haworth's chauvinistic writings of the time:

> *Women's minds were found comparatively inactive in the later period of gestation, especially those who had not yet reached their full physical maturity. Though heavier classics and books were added to the library to add a variety of greater educational and inspirational value for the occasional client.*

In 1924 the Haworth's purchased a fifty-foot lot on the south side of the main building. This area was fenced in and became an outside recreation area for the pleasure of the patients. It was called "the bullpen" and included a garden with an oval walk where girls could escape to get some fresh air when weather permitted. Until The Willows closed, benches beside the oval walk became the favorite place for the girls to spend days in the warm sun, feeding the squirrels.

"The Bullpen" 1928

"The Bullpen" 1934
The Patients' Outdoor Secluded Recreation Park
Photos courtesy of Carol Haworth Price

There were two dining rooms, one for the girls still with child and the other for the girls who had delivered their babies. When a girl became "sick" or went into labor, she was taken to one of the Confinement Rooms. After giving birth, she was moved to another area of the facility called the Convalescence Area, never again to see the others who were still waiting to give birth. Presumably they didn't want the new mothers to share details of the act of giving birth, frightening those still pregnant.

The Willows had a large nursery for the new infants. At its maximum capacity, it was said to have held as many as 125 babies at a time. In a 1925 brochure, it shows there was a large, open-air, roof-garden nursery where babies were kept during summer months. Another article said it was where ill babies were kept. In later years, there was a large outdoor nursery tent on the grounds for the infants to experience the fresh Kansas City air.

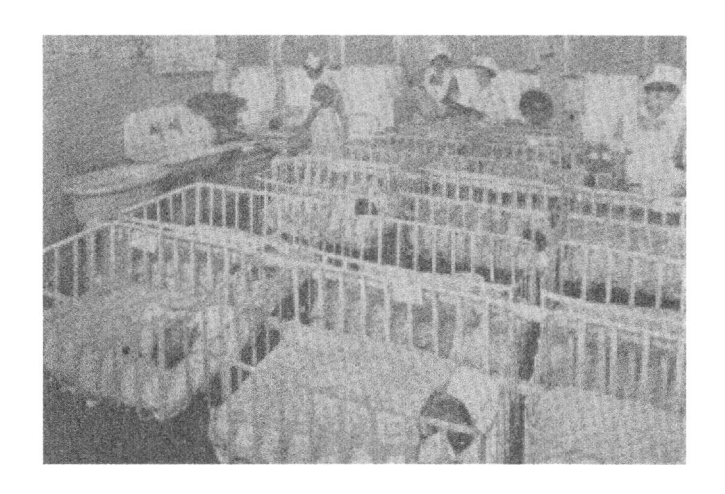

The Crèche Nursery and The Roof Garden Nursery
Photos courtesy of Carol Haworth Price

There were examination rooms where a resident house doctor would give the girls routine checkups. Dr. John W. Kepner was the resident doctor from 1905 until 1931. He helped the Haworths start The Willows. By the year he examined Leona and delivered her baby, he had already delivered over 4,000 Willow babies. Several other doctors over the years were affiliated with The Willows and provided excellent care for the young women and their babies. One past resident from the late 60s noted as a sixteen-year-old girl, the examinations were most embarrassing. To make matters worse and to the dismay of the red-faced girls, often groups of young male interns would be present to observe the doctor's exams. Presumably allowing this training was another source of income that helped fund the home.

Another room many of the girls did not care for was the massage room. To their chagrin, being exposed and having hands on their bodies was more than humiliating. Especially troubling was when those roving hands approached forbidden body parts. The girl being massaged was assured this was for her own interest so when she returned home, any hints of childbirth were removed. Another excerpt from Mr. Haworth's 1918 "By-Paths and Cross-Roads: Accidents of Fair Travelers on the Highway of Life," shared an explanation for this unique massage service the facility offered its clients.

> *Early entrance during gestation is important for preparing the patient for accouchement through systematic hygienic methods and massage. A special system of abdominal and perineal massage has been originated for preventing striae gravidarum (pinkish or purplish, scar-like lesions, later becoming white, on the breasts, thighs, abdomen, and buttocks, due to weakening of elastic tissues, associated with pregnancy) and as an aid to labor. The abdominal markings of a single girl, caused by carrying a child, are telltale signs that might be discovered at any time and cause her misfortune to become known. This combination of massages, including the skin, perineal, and vaginal massage, has been successful in sending numbers of girls, who have taken them, away from The Willows without marks or signs to show of their experience.*

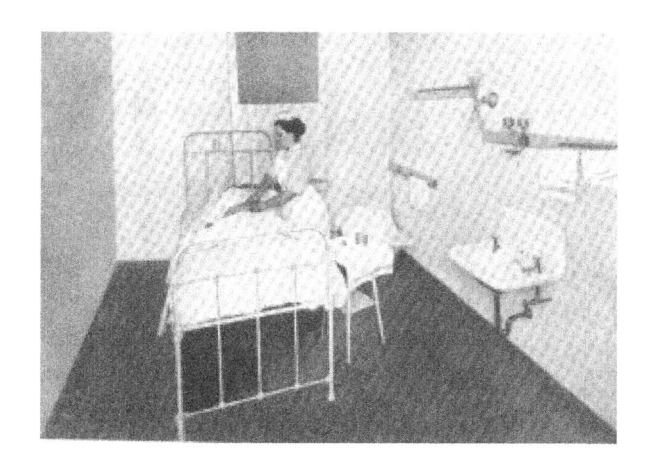

Massage Room
Photo courtesy of Carol Haworth Price

Mr. Haworth, in this document, emphasized to doctors the necessity of sending patients to The Willows as early as possible to enable young women to avoid gossip and social stress. The later in pregnancy a young woman came to The Willows, the more scrutiny placed on her appearance and reason for being gone. Interestingly, he noted the double moral standard set up by society, saying:

> *The double standard as set up by society has forced womankind to undertake every conceivable means to cover up her mistakes from society, knowing full well the catastrophe which would befall her once her secret became known. With her brother flaunting his mistakes in the face of the world and receiving little or no condemnation, can she then be blamed for seeking to protect herself from injustice and suffering from which until recently she had had little or no recourse.*

Leona spent almost four months at The Willows while her baby's father carried on with life unscathed. She arrived on November 17 and "celebrated" her seventeenth birthday on December 27, 1924, seven and a half months pregnant. She would say years later that the time she spent there was a blur. She felt as if she was in a daze the entire time.

The daily routine was always the same. The nurses would go room-to-room, waking the girls to tell them it was time to get up and get ready for breakfast. Breakfast, lunch and dinner were all served in the dining room. Mrs. Haworth was a stickler for promptness. Leona learned quickly to be in her seat on time. The cook prepared delicious, healthy meals for the young women. Nurses' aides and kitchen helpers served the food. A few of the girls whose families didn't have sufficient funds for expenses would help with meals and laundry to pay their way.

Dining Room
Photo courtesy of Carol Haworth Price

Leona's farm girl upbringing had not prepared her for the proper table etiquette Mrs. Haworth expected from "her" girls. She spent time teaching the girls table manners every young woman should know. She thought it was important for the girls to be prepared for society when they returned to their lives outside of The Willows. Mrs. Haworth's Twelve Table Manner Rules included:

MANSION ON A HILL

Rule 1: Place your napkin in your lap immediately upon sitting down. Unfold it while it is in your lap.

Rule 2: In most situations, use the "outside-in" rule to tell which knife, fork, or spoon to use at the dinner table. Use utensils on the outside first and work your way in with each new course.

Rule 3: Food is removed from the mouth in the manner in which it is put into the mouth. Food put into the mouth with a utensil is removed with a utensil.

Rule 4: When fingers are used to eat food, the pit or bone is removed with fingers.

Rule 5: Simply say "excuse me, please; I'll be right back" when leaving for the restroom. Leaving without a word is rude.

Rule 6: Cut your food into only one or two bite-sized pieces at a time. If you have more than a few words to say, swallow your food, rest your fork on your plate, and speak before you resume eating.

Rule 7: Scraping a plate or loudly chewing is unpleasant to listen to and considered impolite. Smacking and slurping food are major mistakes and a sign of bad table manners.

Rule 8: In formal dining the knife is used to push food against the fork. At informal meals, a knife or a piece of bread is used as a pusher, for example, to push salad onto a fork.

Rule 9: The "no elbows on the table" rule applies only when you are actually eating. When no utensils are being used, putting your elbows on the table is acceptable.

Rule 10: When food is caught between the teeth that is annoying or uncomfortable, wait to remove it privately.

Rule 11: When holding a utensil, rest your other hand in your lap. When not holding any utensils, both hands remain in the lap.

Rule 12: Do not fidget, and always keep your hands away from your hair. Do not hunch your shoulders over your plate. Likewise, slouching back in your chair (which makes it look as if you're not interested in the meal) is bad table manners.

Mrs. E. P. Haworth, Superintendent 1934
Photo courtesy of Carol Haworth Price

MANSION ON A HILL

After breakfast, girls were expected to go back to their rooms to tidy up. They could spend the day in the parlor or library. Leona loved playing games and often played checkers or cards with other girls. She also liked to read. She loved music and enjoyed when girls played the piano or other instruments. She wished she could play.

Every day one of the nurses would check on Leona's physical condition. They would check her weight, check her pulse, and see if there were any aches or pains. At least once a week, Dr. Kepner would examine Leona to make sure she was progressing well. Leona loved Dr. Kepner. He treated her with respect and showed he cared. He reminded Leona of her daddy, who had passed away from influenza when she was just a little girl. She missed him so much.

Like the other girls, Leona did not enjoy or appreciate the massages she was given. As a sixteen-year-old farm girl, the notion of getting a massage was as foreign to her as buying a new dress like the one in the magazine ad she saw for the new Saks Fifth Avenue in New York City. However, The Willows nurses giving her massages were very gentle and explained how the treatment would help her body not to have stretch marks. It would hide signs of having been pregnant. Nevertheless, it was embarrassing.

In the afternoons when the weather was not too cold, Leona loved getting outdoors. The farm girl in her hated being cooped up. She enjoyed going out to "the bullpen" where she could walk around the oval or sit on the bench and feed the squirrels. It was a wonderful retreat, which reminded her of home.

Leona was homesick the entire time she was at The Willows. Days stretched into weeks and weeks into months. When the girls moved into The Willows, they often used alias first names and did not share their last names to protect their identities from one another. Leona didn't care and used her real first name. Her roommate went by Dot, but Leona knew that really wasn't her name. Leona felt a comradery with many of the other girls. The girls were all there for the same reason so they understood and consoled one another. Mrs. Haworth and the staff members were strict but treated them with respect and not as social lepers. They encouraged the young women to make something out of their lives after they left The Willows. It was stressed to the girls that they were getting a second chance.

Leona never forgot the day she went into labor. Several girls before her had gotten "sick" and were taken to the white, sterile confinement room. When it was her turn, fear consumed her. After her water broke, Leona was moved into confinement. She would spend the entire day in labor before her baby girl was delivered. Mrs. Haworth and nurses took turns staying with Leona, comforting her through a painful delivery. Dr. Kepner delivered her baby girl at 7:55 p.m. on Valentine's Day, February 14, 1925. She would remember for the rest of her life the kindness and care Mrs. Haworth, the nurses, and the doctor showed to her that day.

The name Leona gave her little Valentine was Marcia. She was a beautiful little girl. While still in the confinement delivery room, Leona nursed her baby for the first time. After nursing, her daughter was taken to the nursery to join the other babies in cribs aligned in rows. In the early years of The Willows, mothers were allowed to nurse their babies as this proved to help the babies to get off to a good start. Toward the end of The Willows operations, mothers were only allowed an hour to hold and rock their babies. Leona was moved to the section of the convalescence floor where those stayed who had delivered their babies. Once there, she wouldn't again see any of her friends who were still pregnant.

Chapter 9

Infamous Adoption at The Willows

During the time Leona was residing at The Willows, she knew nothing of the turmoil that embroiled The Willows. A national scandal hit the papers across America in 1924, which led Mr. Haworth to make additional policy changes when it came to parents seeking to adopt a baby.

Lydia Locke, also known as Lady Talbot, was a famous opera singer in the early 1900s. Originally from Hannibal, Missouri, she found fame and fortune with her beautiful voice. It provided her the opportunity to travel the world. She was also well known in the tabloids for her seven rocky marriages. Her first marriage to Lord Reginald W. Talbot ended in divorce due to spousal abuse claims. While meeting with a divorce lawyer, during an argument Lydia shot him with the pistol she had hidden in her fur muff. Though tried for murder, the shooting was said to be accidental and she was found innocent.

Lady Lydia Locke Talbot in 1910 at age 26

Her second marriage began just as shakily when Lydia "accidentally" fired a gun at her husband on their honeymoon but missed. They remained together for a few years but later divorced after several court appearances.

Husband three, Lieutenant Commander Arthur Marks, was the marriage in which Lydia brought The Willows into play. This marriage was Lydia's longest, lasting six years. He was a wealthy former executive of the B. F. Goodrich tire company and the president of an organ company at the time of their marriage in 1918. During their marriage, the couple adopted a son, but the little family soon unraveled.

There was an article titled "Like a 'Vamp' in the Movies" in the November 8, 1925, *San Antonio Light* newspaper that told the story of the Marks' family melodrama.[18]

> **Like a "Vamp" in the Movies**
>
> Startling Exploits and Experiences in the Restless Career of Lydia Locke, Who Shot One Husband, Divorced Two, Plotted With a Bogus Baby and Is Before the Courts Once More
>
> Attractive Photograph of Lydia Locke-Talbot-Harrold-Marks-Dornblasser.
>
> Nov. 8, 1925

According to the article, Mr. Marks was checked into a sanitarium with signs of extreme fatigue. Lydia called persistently to the hospital and the staff deflected her calls. Marks' doctor told him he had better pack up. They can't do anything for him. What he needed was a divorce.

It appears Marks agreed and filed for divorce in 1924, settling by giving Lydia properties and $300,000. After their divorce, Lydia continued to harass Marks, calling night and day. He offered her an additional $100,000 if she didn't contact him for a year, and she took the bribe. But after six months, Locke was back in Marks' life. She had a new baby and claimed it was his. Marks believed her at first and took financial responsibility for the child. Wary of the strange time frame, he hired private detectives to look into the birth. They discovered that Lydia had not given birth but had adopted the infant boy from The Willows Maternity Sanitarium in Kansas City under the assumed name "Mrs. Ira Johnson." She said she was from Hannibal, Missouri, with papers establishing herself as a woman of responsibility. An article from *The Washington Post* dated, November 11, 1924 gives more detail.

KELLEE PARR

FORMER LADY TALBOT CONFESSES BABY PLOT
Alleged Son Of Third Husband Was Asylum Waif, She Admits In Court

New York, Nov. 10—A six-weeks old boy – a waif from Kansas City, Mo. – was the chief actor in a domestic drama, revealed before **Supreme Court Justice Gavegan** today, that had as its main theme the deception of a wealthy former husband.

Confronted by evidence gathered in Kansas City, St. Louis and Hannibal, Mo., **Mrs. Lydia Locke Marks** admitted that she had obtained the baby under false pretenses and brought him here in an attempt to persuade the husband she recently divorced that the child was hers and that he was the father.

Her former husband, **Arthur Hudson Marks**, millionaire organ and automobile tire manufacturer, was responsible for today's court action, which ended with an order for the return of the child to **The Willows Sanitarium** in Kansas City.[19]

The baby was returned to The Willows by authorities. Locke was not formally charged with any wrongdoing. This court case would have been going on during the time Leona was living at The Willows, though the girls in the home never knew about it. They would have feared their babies would be abused in such a manner instead of being placed with proper families as promised. Locke's deception led to terrible publicity so the Haworths put a rule in place that both prospective parents had to be present to adopt.

Chapter 10

Leaving The Willows

It was the same ending of the story for every single girl who entered The Willows. Once the baby was delivered, it was time to leave for home. Time to return to society, heartbroken with a secret to carry the rest of her life.

Leona was just one of tens of thousands of Willows' girls. She delivered her baby on Valentine's Day and was taken to a recovery room. She and her baby Marcia were tested for any social diseases. The results came back negative on February 24. If they had been positive, she and her baby would have been sent home together. The paperwork relinquishing her rights to Marcia was signed. Mrs. Haworth told Leona after three weeks of recuperation that it was time for her to head home. She was encouraged to never look for her baby. It was best for the baby and the adoptive family to not interfere with their lives.

Leona was devastated. She felt hollow inside on that cold March day in 1925 when she left The Willows and was taken to the Union Station train depot. Mrs. Haworth purchased a ticket for her, but instead of returning to Independence, Leona's destination was Garnett, Kansas, where her sister Iva lived. As Leona heard the call for all aboard, Mrs. Haworth patted her on the hand and reassured her that she had made the right decision in coming to The Willows. She told Leona they would find a wonderful home for her baby and she felt she knew exactly the perfect couple to raise her. They were a farm couple who had already adopted a son from The Willows. Leona said thank you, but this good news did little to cheer her. She put on a brave face and half-smiled at Mrs. Haworth, who gave her a hug before Leona climbed the steps up onto the train. She felt that not only had she left her baby girl behind but her heart as well.

    It was much lonelier without Louis on her second train ride. She clutched her stomach feeling the loss of the baby she had carried for so long. At least no one had been able to take Leona's baby from her as long as she was carrying her inside. She had found a seat by the window. Leona looked out as the train passed through the city and slowly made its way to open land. She could not look at anyone else on the train and focused on the scenes passing by or kept her eyes shut.

    When she arrived at her destination, Iva was there to greet her. Leona saw her wave as the train pulled to a stop. Leona gathered her small bag of belongings, slipped on the coat that had been over her shoulders, and folded over her arm the lap blanket her mother had sent with her last November. She made her way down the aisle, avoiding eye contact. The conductor held her hand as she climbed down the steps to the platform where Iva was waiting to give her a huge hug. Iva's little five-year-old daughter, Lola, was with her. Lola hugged her Aunt Ona, who was wearing the like-new, blue gingham dress that she had only worn once, the day she went to The Willows. Leona's body was still healing from childbirth, but to look at her, no one would have known. Maybe those massages had helped. The nurses at The Willows had wrapped Leona's breasts tight with fabric to help with the swelling from lactation and lack of nursing. It was so uncomfortable, but the nurses said to keep them on for at least a week to ten days until she quit lactating. Little did they know at the time, this was probably the worst thing they could have told the women to do as it could result in plugged ducts and mastitis.

    With her arm around Leona and tears in her eyes, Iva guided Leona to her husband's awaiting car to take her to their home. Iva was careful not to ask her any questions about the birth within earshot of Lola. This family secret was one Lola didn't need to know. Iva shared all the family news that had happened during the time Leona was away. Mama was okay but heartbroken while Leona was gone. Louis was doing well and still helping with the farm, but times were tough. Goldie missed her dearly but was doing great in school. And last time they visited, Bud had shot a skunk down at the creek and smelled to high heaven.

Leona stayed with Iva for a couple months. For several days, she didn't have much to say. She didn't want to leave her room. Iva never saw Leona cry, but she knew she did. She was melancholy, and Iva worried her sister would never come out of this depression. It took Leona quite some time to get back to living her normal life. Day-by-day as her body healed, she gradually became her old self. Iva and her family were loving and caring. They were in no hurry for her to leave. Lola and Leona developed a lifelong bond through this time spent together.

One day they received word that Grams was very ill. They loaded up the car and made the trip to the farm in Havana. It was so good to see Mama, Louis, Goldie and Bud. The first time Bud saw his "Ona," he ran and grabbed her around the waist. He didn't want to let her go. A tear formed in the corner of her eye. Leona was glad she had spent the time with Iva to recuperate because she knew she would have been a crying mess if she had gone straight home from The Willows and seen her mama and siblings.

Leona tiptoed into Grams' room. Grams appeared to be sleeping. The creak in the floor board gave Leona's presence away. "Come here child," Grams said to her granddaughter. "Let me look at you."

She reached up with her shaking arms toward Leona and the two embraced. It was the best hug ever. One Leona had longed for the past six months. Not a word was spoken about Leona's ordeal, but the tear in the corner of Gram's eye said it all. She knew what strife Leona had been through and that she was still suffering. She knew Leona's life would move on. The pain would lessen, but it would never go away. The subject of baby Marcia or The Willows was never discussed with Gram or any of the family. It was as if it never happened. They were just happy to have their "Ona" back home.

Chapter 11

Sixty-four Years of Operation

During sixty-four years of operation, The Willows grew and evolved with the times while maintaining its original goal of providing refuge for the unfortunate girls who passed through its door. Over the years many changes took place to the building and the operations of The Willows.

The Haworths owned the entire block from Main to Walnut Streets between 29th and 30th Streets. E. P. Haworth made a brilliant move when he added a nursing school, which was located just east of The Willows Maternity Hospital. It was opened within the first few years of The Willows operation. It is assumed to have been born out of necessity to meet the demand for good nurses to care for the young mothers and their infants.

Brochure "Training School for Obstetric and Infant Nursing" for The Willows Nursing School

In 1910 The Willows Nursing School educated young women to become nurses through a twelve-month course. By 1912 they bumped up the training to a fourteen-month course to continue to provide the best training possible. Originally, they just advertised for student nurses in local papers. But with the start of *The Willows Magazine* in 1911, applicants came from all over the country. For The Willows, the student nurses helped provide the necessary staffing to take care of the infants. The school also provided income for The Willows through tuition. Kansas City benefited by having trained nurses looking for work in other facilities and hospitals upon graduation. Until a new addition was added in 1911, nurses who worked at The Willows slept in a large tent while patients were accommodated in the main house. Records do not indicate when the school closed. The Haworth's granddaughter Carol Price Haworth doesn't know for certain how long the nursing school was open but doesn't think it was very long.

MANSION ON A HILL

The Willows in 1910
The Nurses Tent, on the right

Nurses from 1924

The Nurses Cottage and Recreation Area Playing Croquet 1929
Photos courtesy of Carol Haworth Price

The 1911 red brick addition increased the adult patient capacity to fifty. The nursery could hold forty-five babies. In later years, the original white, wooden building was redone with a distinguished red brick facade to match the addition.

After World War I, there was a decline in business and adjustments were necessary to meet the changing economic situation. But by 1925, business was booming and plans were made to enlarge the facility to meet the demand in all areas of service. Additional cottages and an annex were added to house the young women. The cottages were often used to house those patients who were not financially able to meet the expense of the main sanitarium home.

The Cottages
Photo courtesy of Carol Haworth Price

In the 1950s, The Willows reached peak capacity with 102 patients. The nursery was full with 134 babies. Years later as number dwindled, only the main building was utilized, according to the Haworth's granddaughter.

In brochures sent to doctors across the country, photographs proudly displayed the various rooms in the facility. Photos showed the patients' tidy bedrooms, the lobby, general reception room, parlor, library, superintendent's office, clerical offices, mailing room for advertising, office for receiving patients, nurses' classroom, drug room, doctor's clean-up room, lobby bath and shower, massage room, confinement chamber, nursery service room, roof garden nursery, house tent, diet kitchen, main dining room, food storeroom, heavy food storeroom, milk kitchen, and nursery refrigerator.

Patients' Room in 1934

Dining Room in 1921

Dining Room in the 40s

Diet Kitchen 1929

Kitchen 1929

Drug Room 1929

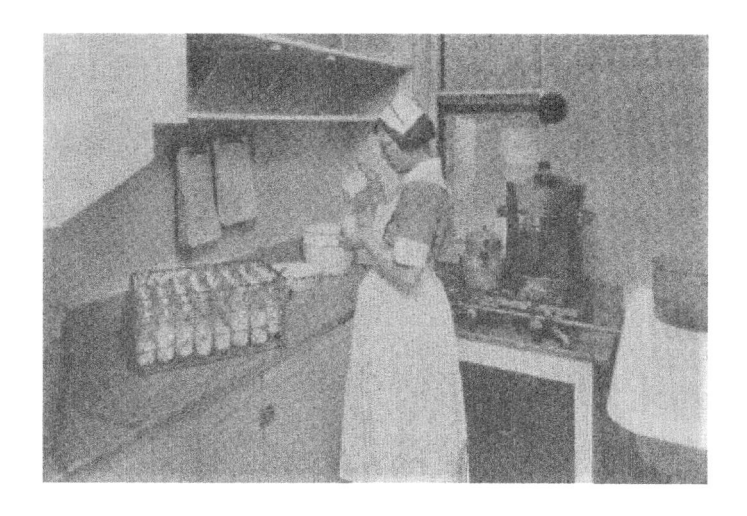

Milk Room 1929

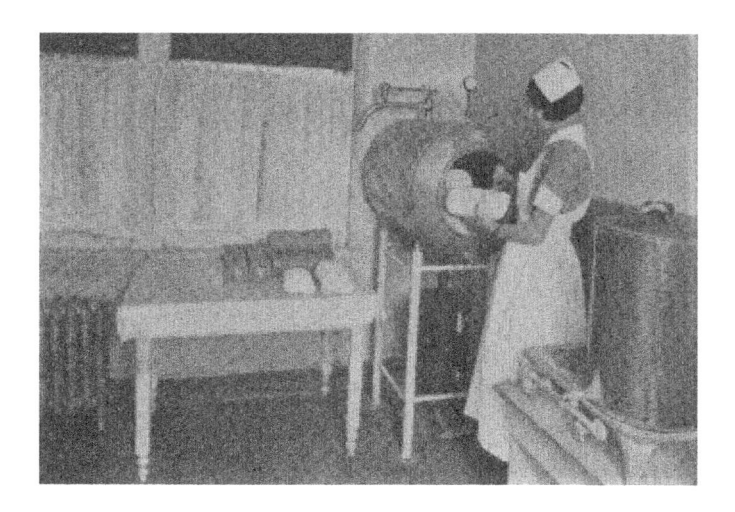

Sanitation Room 1929
Photos courtesy of Carol Haworth Price

The staff needed to run The Willows increased in numbers over the years in relation to the facility's increased size and number of residents. In 1910 there were thirty-three employees including: superintendent, assistant superintendent, office manager, secretary, cashier/bookkeeper, stenographer, obstetrician, pediatrician, superintendent of nurses, fourteen student nurses, housekeeper, cook, two dining room girls, floor maid, private cook for superintendent, engineer, porter, and two laundry helpers.

By 1925, the staff had ballooned to fifty-nine workers with six additional student nurses, five additional kitchen and dining room helpers, four more laundry helpers, a telephone operator, a secretary, two more stenographers, a pathologist, night fireman, an additional porter, and a matron of the nurses' home. The staff made the facility run like a well-oiled machine.

Lots of changes were made over the years to the inside of the facility as well as the outside. Prior to 1925 The Willows' laundry facility was quite inadequate. New modern machines were installed to handle the mass quantity of laundry for both the patients and the facility. The entire building was redecorated the same year and new furnishings added. New radios with loudspeakers were provided for the different lobbies. The residents were given the opportunity to hear not only the local radio shows but out-of-town shows as well. It was a nice connection to the outside world while they were in seclusion.

From the beginning of the maternity home, Mr. Haworth wrote about and advertised the importance of The Willows being a seclusion residence. He believed the girls should not be seen or interact with the outside world for the young women's protection. He thought if girls were out and about, one would never know when a young woman might encounter someone she knew. Her secret would be revealed and reputation destroyed.

A Willows' patient from 1946 stated the girls were not allowed to leave the grounds unless family came to visit. She was told they were isolated from society to protect them from the contempt of the outside world. Similar to what Leona experienced in the 20s, her only exposure to people outside The Willows was looking out her bedroom window at the street far below the hill. Another resident from the 40s noted that a few "privileged" girls worked in the office. By privileged she meant they got to see people from the outside, while the other residents were not allowed to interact with outsiders.

To meet the girls' necessities and avoid the need to venture out into public, The Willows had a store for the girls to purchase things, such as toothpaste, stationary, pens, paper, and the like. The store was still in operation at The Willows' closing.

The seclusion philosophy began to shift in the 1950s. With a change of ownership, the management and direction of the house evolved with the times, but one thing never changed. This was the commitment to provide privacy and a safe haven for their girls. Garnet "Peggy" Haworth (who was married to E. P. and Cora Haworth's son Don) purchased The Willows and took over the role of superintendent in 1953 after her mother-in-law's death.

Donald David Haworth (E.P. and Cora's son)
Don and Garnet "Peggy" Haworth
Photos courtesy of Carol Haworth Price

Garnet was known outside The Willows by her nickname Peggy. But anything dealing with the maternity home, she was called Garnet. The girls in the home referred to her as "Mrs. H." and themselves as "Garnet's girls." She adored her mother-in-law and felt it a true privilege to carry on her legacy. Garnet's daughter Carol noted it was amazing how dedicated her mother was to the girls. Her mother felt as if the girls were her own. Garnet spent endless hours with them from the time they arrived, through the delivery of their babies, and until they went home. She even kept in touch with many of the girls years later.

As societal norms and expectations changed, so did the restrictions for the girls, especially after Garnet took over as superintendent. The rules became less strict. The girls were given more freedom to take day trips away from the home – a far cry from when Leona was told to keep the curtain closed and never to look out the windows.

In the late 1950s, the girls were allowed to go out once a week up until their ninth month of pregnancy as long as they were with another girl. In their last month, they could only go out with a nurse. The girls could order out from a nearby ice cream parlor or custard stand, but no more than once a week to maintain a healthy diet and to avoid too much weight gain. There was no lights-out curfew although girls were encouraged to be in bed and quiet after a certain hour. Everyone was expected to be at meals, but some girls with particularly sensitive stomachs or a tinge of attitude often had meals brought to their rooms by nurses.

The girls were still expected to change the bed linens and take their dirty laundry downstairs once a week. Though now, their laundry was done for them. Another change was The Willows had a pay phone and the girls could make as many phone calls as they wanted without having to have permission. If the pay phone rang, only a nurse was allowed to answer. She would page the girl the call was for to let her know there was an incoming call. One can only imagine how badly Leona would have loved to have had that line of communication with her family when she was a resident.

There were a few private rooms, but most girls shared a room with one or two roommates. One private room had wallpaper with little pink roses and had been furnished with French provincial furniture. One girl was told this had been Mrs. Haworth's daughter's furniture when she was young. The girls in predelivery dined in the basement. This dining room had plastic couches along the wall for the girls to sit while they waited for meals. They hated sitting on these couches with legs sticking to them when they stood up.

As in the early years of The Willows, the girls were taught to knit and crochet. Many a sweater was made for the boyfriend back home. They also had a television set to watch shows and the TV room became a favorite gathering place. A few girls even had TVs in their rooms. Over all, the girls felt they were treated very well under such trying emotional circumstances.

In the 1960s The Plaza and Downtown Mall were favorite places to go to shop and eat. Girls were known to purchase dime store wedding bands and slip them on their fingers before going out in public to ward off questions about being pregnant and unmarried. The girls were given strict guidelines about outside trips from The Willows. They were to check out with one of the nurses before leaving and were never to go out alone. Strict curfews were set for returning and girls were to sign back in with staff. However, as one of The Willows' residents said, "Rules were meant to be broken."

There were consequences like loss of privileges when girls were tardy in returning or broke other rules. Boredom sometimes got the girls into trouble. A story shared by a 1960s resident said three girls got in trouble for stealing ice cream cups out of the freezer. One of them had snatched a random "lost" key to the freezer room. The girls would sneak in at night to eat ice cream. That is – until they were caught and had to return the key!

It is overwhelming to imagine being in charge of up to one hundred pregnant, teenage girls to mid-twenty-year-old young women with different backgrounds and personalities. Homesickness, stress, fear, loneliness, aching bodies, and changing hormones all caused confusing mixed emotions. One has to assume there were plenty of attitude issues from some of the girls who were used to being pampered. It took very special people to operate such a home, having lots of patience and love to provide services for such a wide range of personalities and needs.

Years after residing at The Willows, women who had stayed there were haunted by memories. In Leona's case, she was hesitant to bring up her stay. She said she had pretty much blocked out that time as it was too painful to remember. The one thing she did say about The Willows was that she was treated well while she stayed there. Though it was a painful experience, she was thankful they had helped her and were kind to her.

One past resident noted that it was funny how certain things trigger recollections of The Willows. She and several other girls shared that the smell of Lysol* is one thing that brings back a flood of memories. Nurses told the girls they had to take a bath before they could see their babies. Girls were issued small bottles of Lysol and expected to use it to clean out the bathtub before they took their baths. One woman said to this day she will put a capful of Lysol in with her towels to wash them. It is one of her favorite smells. All these years later, the scent always reminds her of her baby, rocking and loving him before she had to leave and return home empty handed.

The Willows Maternity Hospital closed its doors in 1969. Garnet's daughter Carol said, "The Willows closed due to a smaller group of patients. They needed more patients in order to make enough money to adequately care for the girls, although they did not lack for excellent care up until the end." She added, "In addition, Mom really wanted to slow down as she was in her mid-60s by then."

In 1969 when The Willows was closed, the house and land were sold to the Hallmark company. The company headquarters is housed a few blocks to the north at Crown Center. In the 1990s, a Residence Inn was located where The Willows once stood and today it is an apartment complex.

MANSION ON A HILL

To this day, rumors and innuendos swirl around The Willows and the Haworth family who operated it. Carol is aware of these and wished to clarify many of the falsehoods circulated. First is the rumor that babies were sold to the wealthy. Carol said, "My grandparents and parents never 'sold' babies to make a profit. That never happened. They only received payment for the young women's stay. They were allowed to charge the adopting families for the blood tests done on the mother and baby, for milk and other supplies for the trip home, and for court costs they incurred. Nothing else."

There is also a rumor that all the records were taken into the backyard and burned in a bonfire after the closing. Carol said that isn't what happened. Her mother and the staff had tried to get the county courts to take the records. They didn't want them because they had no place to put them. Feeling the need to respect and honor the privacy promised to their patients over all the years, the records were taken to the Federal Reserve and they destroyed them. Items such as old brochures and marketing pieces were given to the Kansas City Historical Society. The only thing Garnet kept, and Carol still has is the large record book her grandmother started at the very beginning. It includes the name of every baby born at The Willows, the date of birth, and vital statistics. Leona's baby was recorded as "baby girl Marcia, born 2/14/25, 8# 7:55 p.m."

Chapter 12

End of an Era

The closing of The Willows was the end of an era. In secrecy, over 35,000 babies were born at the facility. Young women from all over the United States and the world were aided at a time of desperation. Each circumstance was different. Some girls were there because they wanted to be but most because they had no choice. It is reported by some residents that there were girls who came back a second time. There are even documented cases of adoptee babies having grown up and gotten pregnant out of wedlock to be sent to The Willows to also give up a baby for adoption. It makes sense that the family of the adoptee would know where to send a daughter found to be in the same circumstance as her biological mother.

Hundreds of thousands of lives were touched and influenced by The Willows and the other "Adoption Hub of America" homes for unwed mothers in Kansas City. The lives of the young women (who left without their babies) and the young adoptive couples (who went home with babies in their arms) were never the same. With over 100,000 babies born in Kansas City, it is hard to fathom how this secret has been so well kept from society and history books. Except for the fact most women, like Leona, never shared with anyone other than a few family members that they had given birth out of wedlock or spent any time at The Willows. Their secrets are buried deep.

MANSION ON A HILL

Times have changed and many of The Willows' confidential matters are being unlocked. Recent ease of access to DNA testing, Internet search availability, and changes in adoption laws have opened many doors that seemed shut forever. As Missouri laws changed in 2016, adoptees longing to know names were finally able to get their original birth certificates (OBC) with a birth mother's name and sometimes the father's name. Many biological mothers have said they did not give the name of the father, leaving the name blank and in some cases even giving a fictitious name to protect the father for whatever reason. Also, often on the OBC are the names of the birth parents' hometowns and occupations, providing more leads for those seeking answers.

With names and hometowns in hand, Internet searches and social media groups have allowed adoptees to find previously unknown relatives so much easier than in the days when search angels were about the only available answer. Even locating and seeing photos of the gravesite of a long-lost relative is possible today through websites, such as Find a Grave™. In addition, inexpensive DNA tests through companies, such as AncestryDNA® and 23andMe®, are connecting family members who never knew the other existed. More and more biological parents and their now adult children are being reunited.

Some people cannot understand the burning desire, and even need, of those who want to know their birth parents. Or that of a mother who yearns to know that her baby is okay and has had a good life. Only those who have felt that separation and "need to know" can truly understand. Adoptees struggle with the desire to know who they are, where they came from, why they were given up for adoption, and their health histories. At the same time, an adopted child fears he or she will be interrupting the biological mother's life and family. The question "Does she even want me to find her?" resonates in every single adoptee's heart. There is also the fear and guilt of the "need to know" hurting the adoptive parents. It is interesting how many adoptees wait until their adoptive parents are no longer living to begin their search, often to find it is too late because their biological mother has also passed away.

At the same time, many biological mothers suffer from deep feelings of guilt and regret. Usually a birth mother had to promise never to look for her adopted child. If she does search for her lost child, she has the same reservations and fear of rejection that adoptees have in their search. She does not want to cause turmoil or disrupt her child's life. The questions "Does she even want to know who I am?" and "Will he resent me that I gave him away?" are always in the back of her mind.

The dilemma is real and daunting. Many adoptees have dealt with this struggle their entire lives. At the same time, there are those adoptees who have no desire whatsoever to know about their biological parents, which is perfectly okay. As far as they are concerned, their adopted parents raised them and are their parents, end of story.

When connections are made, each reunion is as unique as the individuals involved. Some adoptive parents or adoptees are thrilled when found, and others have no interest in developing a relationship with this stranger who came looking. Not all reunions have happy results, but from hearing about the ones that do, the search is definitely worth it. Whoever is on the searching side must be prepared for the possibility of rejection and disappointment. One needs to proceed with caution and sensitivity for both parties involved. The smallest of things one wouldn't think of can be quite overwhelming. For example, Leona named her baby Marcia. The only other thing besides life she was able to give to her daughter was her name. Leona had carried that name in her heart all of her years. Imagine what it might be like for a birth mother to be reunited with a child only to find out the name was changed. It could be quite heartbreaking.

As more reunions are made and other searches continue, tens of thousands of women and babies across the country have one thing in common, The Willows Maternity Sanitarium. All the women who resided at The Willows and all those born at The Willows had their

MANSION ON A HILL

lives touched and changed forever because of the Haworth family. The Haworths had a vision to help young women in trouble and families wanting to adopt a child. They devoted their lives to The Willows for sixty-four years, loving and caring for young women and babies who needed their help.

Part Two

Voices of The Willows

The following are stories of those whose lives were touched by The Willows Maternity Sanitarium. There are many similarities to Leona's experience, and each has its own heartfelt connection to The Willows.

Most of these anecdotes are about searching for answers. People who wanted to know the "who" and "why" to their past. These "Voices of The Willows" share that happy endings are possible. For those still looking, it is true that some searches do not provide answers or turn into the results desired. One must be prepared that there might be reactions of resistance, awkwardness, displeasure, and possibly outright denial, all leading to huge disappointment. Hopefully these stories will encourage adoptees who question the "who" and "why" to follow their hearts and know the search can be worthwhile. Never give up hope.

Chapter 13

Linda's Story
(1925)

Linda's story is very similar to mine. We are both grandchildren of women who gave birth at The Willows. We both wanted to learn more about our heritage and searched to find answers. However, Linda's mother was not interested in learning about her biological mother, while my mother had always yearned to know more. Amazingly Linda's mother was born just six days before Leona had her baby. Her biological grandmother and Leona would have known each other.

My mother was born at the Willows Maternity Sanitarium on February 8, 1925. She was adopted by Charles and Bessie Kretzinger when she was five weeks old. Her biological mother had named her Edna, which my grandparents kept as her legal adopted name.

Linda's mother, Edna Kretzinger
Photo courtesy of Linda Palmer

My mother Edna always knew she was adopted, but that was the only information she was allowed to know. She grew up an only child in a small town called Minden Mines, Missouri. Her parents corresponded with The Willows through letters, requesting to adopt a blue-eyed baby girl. The Willows responded to their request with information about a baby girl that they recommended for their home. They were told baby Edna was one month old with brown hair and brown eyes. The letter went on to say that "We note that your preference is a blue-eyed baby, but we do not believe you will let the small matter of color of eyes stand in the way of your getting a nice little girl."

I was always curious about my heritage and my biological grandmother. My mother told me she felt abandoned and was not interested in knowing who her mother was, but I was welcome to see what information I could find. She gave me all of the documents and correspondence that she found in my grandparents' home after they passed away. My mother's name on the adoption decree was listed as Edna Ocamb.

MANSION ON A HILL

I now had a last name but did not know if it was her birth mother's or her birth father's. I joined a group in Denver called Adoptees in Search. As I received information from the monthly meetings about searching, I was passing this information on to my mother. She decided she was more interested in knowing about her birth parents than she thought. She then joined the Kansas City branch of Adoptees in Search and was able to find that her mother's name was Izetta Ocamb. Izetta had passed away about fifteen years before this, but through Ocamb relatives, we were able to learn more about her life.

Izetta was born around 1900 and lost her hearing at the age of four months from spinal meningitis. Her degree of deafness was listed as total. She attended the Kansas State School for the Deaf at Olathe, Kansas, from 1908 to 1921. Through records from the school, my mother was able to contact school friends of Izetta's. Many provided photos and memories of Izetta's school days. None of her friends knew about my mother's birth.

Izetta (with bows in her hair) at the Kansas School of the Deaf
Photo courtesy of Linda Palmer

Friends of Izetta's remember her mother, Ruth Ocamb, visiting Izetta on weekends and bringing candy for all of her classmates. All of the census information on Ancestry.com lists Izetta and Ruth as sisters, but Ruth is listed as Izetta's mother on the school records. All of Izetta's friends knew Ruth as her mother. Izetta's father is listed as Frank Kellousberg on the school records. It appears that Ruth gave birth to Izetta as a teenager but was known as Ruth's sister for anyone other than close family. After learning about Izetta's deafness, my mother felt a great sadness thinking of Izetta having to give up a baby possibly not by her choice.

I joined Ancestry.com and through DNA testing have learned that I am related to many Ocamb family members, but none knew about Izetta having a baby. She did eventually get married but I didn't find that she had any other children. I wish we would have had the opportunity to meet Izetta. I am sure she would have been happy to meet her daughter.

I still do not have any information on my mother's biological father but hope to request an original birth certificate through the state of Missouri. I have always been "tan" and I can't tell you how many times I have been asked "what nationality are you?" My DNA test results were Great Britain, Ireland, Scotland, Wales plus low confidence regions – Eastern Europe, Iberian Peninsula and European Jewish. Not the outcome I expected. I have heard from several 2nd, 3rd and 4th cousins who are my DNA matches that their ethnicity estimates are Africa, Congo, Ghana, etc. I think the identity of my mother's biological father is the answer.

Here's a little twist to my story. An interesting note about my grandparents. My mother, Edna Kretzinger, married my father, Frank Kretzinger, in 1944. Yes, same last name. Frank's father is Mark Kretzinger. Mark and Charles (Edna's father) were brothers. This would make my parents first cousins but not by blood because my mother was adopted into the Kretzinger family. I always had fun trying to explain that my two grandfathers were brothers.

Linda's grandmother Izetta, left, and Linda, right
Photos courtesy of Linda Palmer

Chapter 14

Esther's Story
(1929)

Esther is a lovely lady I met after she heard me being interviewed on the radio about my book My Little Valentine. *She had been adopted by a western Kansas family in 1929. Her story is very similar to my mother's, growing up in an adoptive family. She contacted the radio station to get information on how to buy my book. It turned out we lived in the same town. After she contacted me, I took her a book and we have become very good friends. Esther recently found more information about her birth parents thanks to the change in the Missouri OBC law. This is her story.*

My parents were from Norton, Kansas. It is a rural farming community in the northwest part of the state. In September of 1929, they went to Kansas City by train to visit my dad's sister and her husband. They lived in Independence, Missouri, and he worked for the postal service. My aunt and uncle had two little girls, and my folks loved spending time with them. My parents had been married four or five years and hadn't been able to have any children. But they loved kids. My parents discussed with their sister and brother-in-law that they didn't appear to be able to have children though they would love to have a child. My uncle said, "Well then, you need to adopt."

MANSION ON A HILL

My folks had been foster parents for a couple of children and hoped to adopt them, but it didn't work out. My uncle said, "I know of a place in Kansas City where you can adopt a child. Let's go."

He took my folks over to this place where they met with the officials there. How they got around all the regulations so easily I don't know. I think it must have been that my uncle was an important person with the post office and knew a lot of people. My folks completed the application and it just happened the facility had some babies available. A couple other babies and I were brought out for them to see from what they told me when I was older. My parents chose me, and they were told to come back the next day to get me. I assume they had to do some checking up on my folks, and that gave them time to do so before I was handed over to them. However, the adoption would not be complete for three months.

My parents went back the next day to take me home. I was three weeks old. They arrived in Kansas City without any notion they would be bringing a baby home with them, but here they were, heading back to Norton by train with me in tow. They had not called ahead back home, and nobody knew they were bringing a baby with them. Talk about a surprise.

From the time I can remember, my parents always told me I was adopted. It was just a part of my life. I knew I had been named Berniece at birth and my last name was Moser. They renamed me Esther. They made sure I knew I had been chosen to be their daughter and that I was very special. I just grew up thinking that was a good way to be and adoption was great.

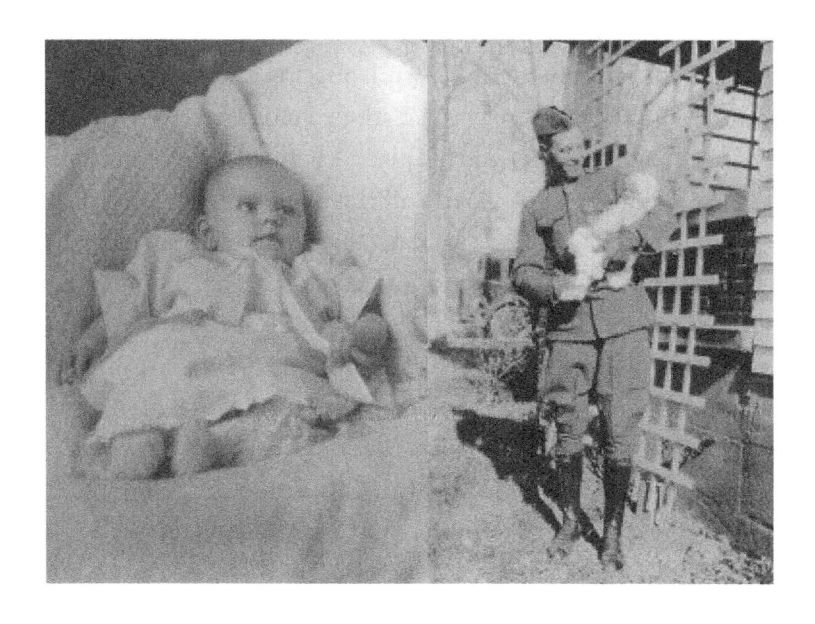

Esther Marie and with her father George Phillips
Photos courtesy of Esther Headrick

When I was in the first or second grade, one day I was walking home with a bunch of my little girlfriends. We stopped at the corner where we would part to go our different ways to our homes. We talked for a bit and one of the little girls said to me in a singsong voice, "We all know something you don't know."

"What?" I said.

"You were adopted."

All the other little girls' mouths were wide open at our brazen friend's announcement.

"Well, I know that," I said.

"You do????"

"Yes, I have always known that."

The little girl said, "Well, how does that make you feel?"

I was a little lost at what the big deal was. I said, "Good, I feel fine."

"Doesn't it make you feel bad?" she asked.

"No, I don't feel bad."

"Well, why not?" she continued to press.

"When you are adopted that means you were chosen," I said. "And if you weren't adopted, you were just had. I was chosen." Continuing in my most proud voice, "My folks looked at more than one baby, and they **chose** me. And when your folks had you, they had **no choice** but to keep you. But **I** was chosen."

The poor little girl got all upset and went home crying. That evening my mother got two or three phone calls from the little girls' mothers asking her to tell Esther to please quit talking about being adopted. My mother told them she didn't realize I did. One mother said, "Well, she certainly did, and my daughter came home today crying."

My mother sat me down and told me that we didn't need any more talk about being adopted. I don't remember which one of my little friends it was that said to me I was adopted, but I went through all grade school and high school with these same friends. I don't ever remember it being brought up again.

In 1932 when I was just about to be three years old, my parents heard from the adoption agency. They had a baby boy available if my parents could come down to Kansas City to see him. It was in July, and my dad worked in the flour mill. It was wheat harvest time, and there was no way he could get away. But my mother and grandmother could go. The agency said that would be okay since they had already met my dad. My mom could sign the papers and take them home for my dad to sign and mail back.

Instead of by train, this time we traveled by car—my mom, my grandma, and me—in our 1929 Chevrolet. I still can't remember the trip. I sure can't fathom what it must have been like for my mom and grandma in the hot July summer. It is almost 350 miles one way. Today it would be over a five-hour trip without stopping. Most of the roads were probably only gravel. No air conditioning. Imagine taking a two-year-old child round trip and bringing home a six-week-old baby who we just met. We went as far as Topeka the first day and stayed with an aunt and uncle who lived there.

The next day we went on to Independence and stayed with my other aunt and uncle. The following day we went to the hospital to see the baby, and I got to go, too. I will NEVER forget that even though I was so little. I was so excited because I was going to get a little brother. I remember some details about the place. My mother and aunts always insisted I was too young to remember anything. One day I finally said to them, "If I describe the building or the house we went into and I am right, then will you believe I remember it?"

"Yes, tell us what it looked like."

"Well, it was big with a large porch and had a big stairway. I was so amazed," I said. "Then the next thing I remember was this little white bundle with a baby they showed us. And that was my little brother."

In astonishment they said that was what the building was like, and they believed I did remember it. After all these years, seeing photos of The Willows I was sure that was the building I remembered. But when I got my original birth certificate, it states that I was born at the Fairmount Hospital in Kansas City. I was a bit disappointed it wasn't The Willows. When I saw photos of the Fairmount building, it didn't look like what I remember from when we went to get my brother. Maybe we went to The Willows and that was where my brother was born. We don't have his records so I don't know where we actually went to adopt him, but in my mind, I think it must have been The Willows.

MANSION ON A HILL

Esther Marie and her brother Gale W. Phillips
Photo courtesy of Esther Headrick

I always wanted to look for my birth mother but also didn't want to cause any hurt feelings for my parents. Now that I have my original birth certificate, I know my mother's name was Bernadine Moser from Kansas City, Missouri. She was twenty-years old and a stenographer. My father's name was Alna Smith from Willow Springs, Missouri. He was twenty-five-years old, and it shows he was an operator for a public service company.

    On the day after Thanksgiving, 2017, my friend who helped me get my original birth certificate called and told me he had some good news. He had looked up Willow Springs on Facebook and found they had a group page. One of his Facebook friends from Topeka went to school in Willow Springs. He asked her if she knew of an Alna Smith, but she didn't. She asked friends on the Willow Springs Facebook group, and one man responded. He did some research and was able to give us information about my birth father. It turned out that Alna Smith was buried in the Willow Springs cemetery. He passed away in 1975. His wife, Bernadine, (yes, the same name as my birth mother) passed away in 1976 and was buried in Forest Lawn Memorial cemetery in Los Angeles, California.

After doing a little research on Ancestry.com, my friend discovered that my birth parents actually got married in the early 1930s after I was born and moved to Hollywood, California. They showed up on the California 1940 census. My mother was actually born in Kansas. In the 1930 Kansas census she shows up as Bernadine Moser and was a stenographer living in Kansas City, Missouri. It appears my birth parents never had any other children. The search for additional relatives continues.

I am thankful for my birth parents giving me life and feel very blessed by my adoption. I could never have asked for a more wonderful family than the one my brother and I were chosen to be a part of all these years.

Esther Marie Phillips Headrick
Photo courtesy of Esther Headrick

Chapter 15

Sue's Story
(1937)

I have so enjoyed getting to know Sue and her husband Frank. Sue shared her wonderful story about her adoption from The Willows and her search for her biological mother. Similar to my mother, Sue has an older brother who was also adopted from The Willows. Sue kept copies of correspondence between her parents and Mrs. Haworth of The Willows. These letters give fascinating insight into the adoption process her family went through. Her parents developed a close relationship with the Haworths over the years.

I was born July 17, 1937, at The Willows and adopted by my parents Cleo and Helene Ingle from Tulsa, Oklahoma. My parents also adopted a boy from The Willows in 1934. They weren't able to have children so they started looking into adoption. My dad had a savings and loan in Tulsa. One of his officers at work was from Kansas and had a relative married into the family of the owners of The Willows. It was the owners' daughter, Ruth Alice, he knew. He told my dad about The Willows and my dad started communicating with them about adopting a son.

In the 1930s, there was a whole group of families in Tulsa who adopted babies from The Willows, including my parents first adopting my brother, Don. My parents informed their family physician, Dr. Hugh Perry, about The Willows. They asked him to inquire about the possibility of adopting a baby. He wrote to The Willows Maternity Sanitarium in November of 1933 requesting an application and catalogue about the facility and their operation.

Mrs. Cora Haworth wrote Dr. Perry back, stating they didn't have any babies for adoption at that time, but my parents could be added to a waiting list. She sent their document called *Album of Willows Babies* that showed photos of adopted babies that were healthy and happy in their new environments. This was Mrs. Haworth's response:

November 8, 1933

Dear Mr. Perry:

We have your letter of November 4th and note that you have patrons contemplating the adoption of a baby. In order to give you and your patrons a better idea as to the type of babies to be found at The Willows, we are mailing under separate cover a copy of our Album of Willows' Babies. The pictures in the album are those of babies after they have been adopted, thus showing how our little ones develop in the home life of the private family.

We have no babies to offer for adoption at this time. The demand for babies of both sexes far exceeds the number available for adoption. People wishing babies find it necessary to go on our waiting list and may have to wait several months for the baby of their choice. We are in a position to give information concerning the parentage of our babies and reasonable assurance that they come from clean, healthy and intelligent parentage.

If your patrons are willing to go on the waiting list, please have them fill in the enclosed blanks and return them to us with three reference letters as directed on back of the blanks. We prefer a reference from their minister, banker and family physician written on the letter heads of the writers and recommending both husband and wife. When we have their completed application, we shall turn it over to our local Court for consideration. When we have the Court's approval we shall notify them and then hold their application until we have a baby to offer them. Our adoption charge is $38.00.

Thanking you for your inquiry and assuring you of our cooperation, we await the arrival of your patrons' completed application.

Fraternally yours,

Mrs. E.P. Haworth, Supt.

THE WILLOWS

Upon completing the application, my dad asked Dr. Perry, District Judge Harry L. S. Halley, banker S. P. McBirney, and minister J. W. Storer, who married my folks two years earlier, to write recommendations. They each gave my parents a glowing report as being potential wonderful parents and provided a copy to my dad for his records. My dad contacted Mrs. Haworth with the application and the following letter:

November 29, 1933

The Willows Nursery

Attention: Mrs. E. P. Haworth, Superintendent

Dear Sirs:

KELLEE PARR

I have your letter of November 8 addressed to Dr. Hugh Perry, which he turned over to me. According to your instructions, we are sending you herewith two application blanks for the adoption of a child. I am also enclosing herewith a recommendation from Judge Harry L. S. Halley, district Judge of the Twenty-first Judicial District; a letter from Dr. Hugh Perry, 417 McBirney Building, this city; a letter from S. P. McBirney, Vice-President of the National Bank of Commerce of this city, and a letter from Dr. J. W. Storer, pastor of the First Baptist Church of this city.

You will note from our application that we prefer a boy with brown eyes, brown hair and one that we can be assured from his heredity that he would grow into the type of manhood that we would desire. We shall endeavor to give him every opportunity to make his place in the world.

We note from your letter to Dr. Perry that you do not have any children for adoption at this time. We would greatly appreciate it if you would give our application due consideration, because we want to state in advance that in all probability we will be a little harder to please than the average prospective foster parents. We will be glad to come to Kansas City at any time that you think you have a suitable child for us and all you need to do is advise us.

We would appreciate it if you would answer this letter and advise us when you think, if possible, you will have a baby that would meet our requirements. For your convenience I am enclosing a self-addressed envelope.

Yours very truly,

MANSION ON A HILL

C. C. Ingle

My parents were notified The Willows had a baby boy for them to adopt named Raymond in early February. My father wrote back:

February 10, 1934

Dear Mrs. Haworth:

I have your letter of February 7 stating that in all probability you will have a baby boy to offer to us for adoption sometime during the current month. In your second paragraph of your letter of the above date, you ask the question if we would be interested in a blue-eyed baby. We would be interested in a blue-eyed baby but we prefer one with brown eyes. In either case, we would like to have a baby whose features are distinct, particularly its eyes and chin. We would like to call your attention to our application stating our size, as we are desirous of having a baby that will grow into a fairly tall man.

We are ready to come at any time you notify us.

Yours very truly,

C. C. Ingle

Upon my parents' further request, Mrs. Haworth sent additional information about baby Raymond:

February 28, 1934

Dear Mrs. Ingle:

In accordance with your recent wire, we are herewith enclosing the history of the parentage of baby Raymond who is now available for adoption.

Baby Raymond, at the present time, has blond hair and his eyes are blue. His head is well formed and his features are good. We cannot, of course be sure that baby Raymond's eyes will be brown but I am sure that he will have dark hair, judging from his parentage. He also has a good chance for brown eyes.

The mother of baby Raymond entered our institution last December and during her stay here, has been a satisfactory patient in every respect. She is of medium build and is of the brunette type. This young woman has been living with her parents who are farmers. She has an older married sister, a brother who is a car salesman and two brothers who are farmers. The family own their farm and are members of a Protestant church. This young woman is by profession a dressmaker.

The father of the baby is doing newspaper work in a small community, although he is a city reared man. His mother and father were accidentally killed in an automobile wreck a few years ago. His father was a newspaper man. This young man is an only child. He also is a member of a Protestant church.

The parents of the baby have known each other for a year and the health record shows no hereditary disease on either side. The Wassermann test on the baby's mother is negative.

Now Mrs. Ingle, if you and Mr. Ingle are interested in baby Raymond, please notify us at once and we shall go ahead with plans to hold him at your disposal until next Tuesday, March 6th. If you arrive here reasonably early that morning, all pro-

cedure can be taken care of so that you may be ready to start home by noon if you care to. It will be satisfactory for you to come by automobile as no doubt the roads are in good condition. If Mr. Ingle cannot come with you, you may come alone as we can send the adoption paper there for his signature after you return home with the baby. You may bring with you a quart Thermos bottle and several nursing bottles or you may obtain them here at the institution.

If for any reason you are not interested in baby Raymond, we wish to make other arrangements for him upon receipt of your communication.

Awaiting your visit, I am

Very truly yours,

Cora M. Haworth

Superintendent

    My parents went by car to Kansas City. When they got there, they were shown baby Raymond. My dad liked the baby, but my mother didn't. She didn't know why, but there was something that made her say she just couldn't take this baby. The Willows had only one other baby boy at the time. He was a premature baby boy born on January 17 who at birth only weighed four pounds and twelve ounces. The staff hadn't planned on showing my parents this baby, but after my mother rejected baby Raymond, they went ahead and brought out baby Eugene. My mother liked him, but my dad didn't. My dad said they would head back to Tulsa and wait for another baby. They started home and my mother cried the whole time. Dad gave in. About halfway home, he turned the car around, and they went back and got this premature baby boy, my older brother Don.

This is the formula The Willows gave to my mom for my brother Don in 1934.

12 ounces Evaporated Milk. 24 Ounces sterile water. 2 tablespoons white Karo Syrup. Feed 5 ounces every 3 hours at 6 am, 9 am, 12 noon, 3 pm. 6 pm, 10 pm, 2 am daily. Warm milk slightly. When baby is six weeks old, give 1 tablespoon orange juice diluted with equal parts sterile water. Give it 1 teaspoon Cod Liver Oil daily before bath in morning. Give 1 or 2 ounces sterile water several times daily. When baby is 3 months old give 1 ounce farina Gruel which has been cooked one hour. Consult your physician as to change or increase in feedings.

After adopting my brother, my parents developed a lifelong relationship with the Haworth family, including their daughter, Ruth Alice. Over the years to follow, my father would stop in and visit the folks at The Willows when he was in town doing business. My parents even invited Mrs. Haworth to our home to stay while attending a hospital convention in Tulsa shortly after Don was brought home. My dad wrote to Mrs. Haworth:

May 12, 1934

Dear Mrs. Haworth:

Mrs. Ingle and I have been so busy with our new arrival that we really have neglected doing a number of things that should be done. If you remember on March 28th, our son, Donald, weighed seven pounds and four ounces and we are exceedingly happy to report that at the present time he weighs ten pounds and nine and one-fourth ounces, and if he continues to gain in the future as he has in the past it, looks like he will take up the whole house. We cannot express to you and your assistant how happy we have been with him and with our selection.

This letter is more an invitation than a dissertation upon the good qualities of our youngster. We have heard nothing further from you and we are still hoping that you expect to come to the hospital convention in Tulsa. Mrs. Ingle and I want to extend to you our best welcome to attend the convention if it is at all possible for you to do so and while here we want you to stay with us and we will do everything possible to make your visit an enjoyable one. We would appreciate it if you could advise us if you are going to attend, and if so, what time we may expect you and we will be delighted to meet you at the train.

Awaiting your response, we are

Yours very truly,

C. C. Ingle

In a return letter written in May 17, 1934, Mrs. Haworth wrote to my parents:

Dear Friends:

I appreciate receiving your nice letter of the 12th and to know that your little son is getting along so splendidly. I am sure that much of his satisfactory development is due to the good care he is receiving in the hands of his foster parents. We know that you will continue to be happy with him.

Your invitation to be your guest, should I attend the Midwest Hospital Convention, gives me a great deal of pleasure and I should surely be delighted to accept. However, I am doubtful as to whether I can attend the convention this year, for business reasons. If I am privileged to go, I shall let you know beforehand, and do thank you many times for your kind invitation.

Wishing you continued success with your little son, I am

Very truly yours,

Cora M. Haworth

It was three years later when my parents adopted me. With them knowing the people at The Willows so well, Mother and Daddy got all kinds of courtesies. Mrs. Haworth acknowledged my parents' application for another baby:

July 13, 1937

Dear Mrs. Ingle:

Just a few lines to tell you that we are today turning over your application to our local Court asking them for an immediate report on your home. When we have the Court's report, we shall notify you and arrange to take care of you as quickly as possible. Enclosed herewith is your receipt for the five-dollar deposit.

Very truly yours,

Cora M. Haworth

I don't know exactly why my parents chose me. As far as I know, my parents didn't know or have any connection to my birth mother.

MANSION ON A HILL

Mrs. Haworth's daughter, Ruth Alice, must have told my mom and dad about this young, unwed mother who was a twenty-year-old student nurse from South Carolina. The story my parents shared with me was that my birth mother, being from the South, couldn't pass the Mason-Dixon Line to the north. Instead, her family looked west and that is why they chose The Willows.

Maybe my great uncle, who was a doctor, had something to do with my parents' decision, and they wanted me because this girl was a nurse. My daddy told me my birth mother was at The Willows for five months before I was born. He said he informed The Willows it didn't matter if I was a girl or a boy, that I was theirs. This is the letter Mrs. Haworth wrote to my mother after I was born. I always laugh at her description of me as a baby. Guess I wasn't a pretty baby. Mrs. Haworth also informed my parents that Dr. Perry, our family physician, could come to Kansas City and interview my birth mother to see if she was of the moral character my family desired. I have never heard of that from anyone else. I don't know if he actually went to interview her or not.

July 26, 1937

Dear Mrs. Ingle:

Today our pediatrician, Dr. Hugh Dwyer, examined a baby girl known here as Esther, and pronounced her normal in every way. Baby Esther is not a pretty baby at this time but has regular features and well-formed head. Her hair is brown and her eyes dark blue. This baby has good parentage and a mother whom we can highly recommend. Since Ruth Alice thinks you may like this baby, she has asked me to write to you about her. If you are interested, we shall give you first opportunity to take her and we shall give Dr. Perry the privilege of personally interviewing this baby's mother. The baby will be two weeks old July 30th, and available for adoption on that day.

KELLEE PARR

The mother of the baby entered our institution last February and while here has been a most satisfactory patient. She has a fair complexion and pretty brown eyes. Her features are good. Her father, a chemist, died a few years ago due to an acute infection. This young woman has a brother in high school and a sister who does kindergarten work. These people have lived in their present community for four years and are members of a Protestant church.

The father of the baby has an office position. His father is a merchant. His people have lived in their present community for 23 years and own their home. The parents of the baby have known each other for about a year and the health record on both sides is good, showing no hereditary diseases nor tuberculosis. The Wassermann test on the baby's mother is negative.

If you are interested in baby Esther, you can let us know at once and we shall then arrange to hold her for you until Friday of this week. Ruth Alice has two other patients in mind for you but they are not expecting confinement until August or September and then, of course, they may have boy babies. We believe you will like baby Esther so we await further word from you.

Very truly yours,

Cora M. Haworth

So, my parents went to Kansas City and brought a second baby home. They changed my name from Esther to Sue. They were wonderful parents. I was so blessed to have a great family. My dad always spoke so highly of The Willows and was so appreciative of the Haworths for helping to bring my brother and me into our family.

Sue Ingle (Esther Wardlaw), left, and with brother Don, right, about 1938
Photos courtesy of Sue Wardlaw Wantland

Mother and Daddy had an antique chest where they kept all the information about our adoption, and we could always look at this any time we wanted. They had a book called *The Chosen Child*. They always said, "We chose you, so feel good."

Sue Ingle after WWII in Tulsa, Oklahoma
Photo courtesy of Sue Wardlaw Wantland

Also, in the chest were the following documents from The Willows that gave information about my brother, Don, and myself. They include a description of parentage.

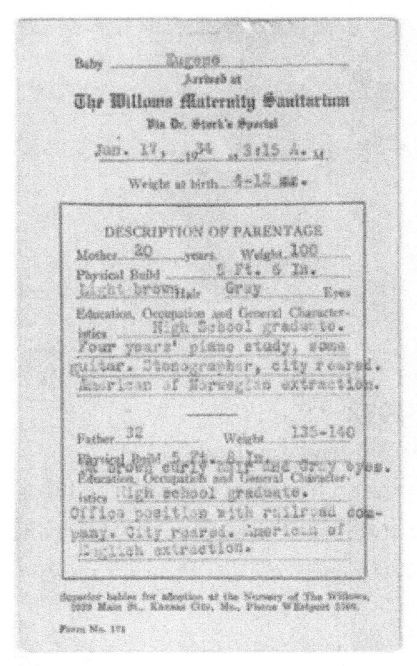

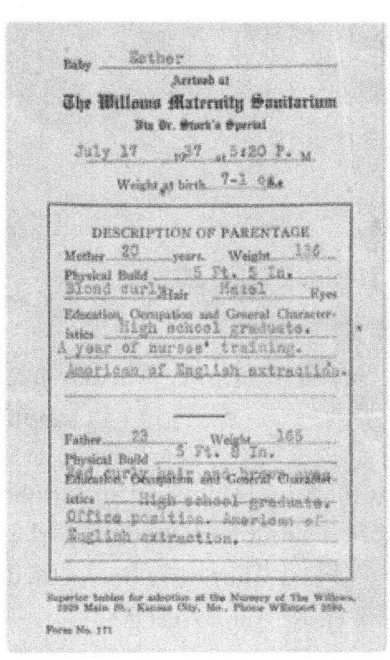

The backs of both documents contain these words of wisdom:

MANSION ON A HILL

"As bends the sapling, so grows the giant oak.

"Tis not the reversal of species, but the development of species the forester seeks and attains.

Pride not yourself that you are better than your humble neighbor, the untutored Ioot, or the depraved Apache. Rather thank the fates that fortune favored you in your education and training during the formative years.

If the royal offspring falls into the hands of the depraved at birth and the child of the gutter occupies the royal cradle, then the royal one is educated a "gutter snipe" and the humble blood grows to be a prince."

Helene, Cleo, Sue and Don Ingle in Washington, DC 1942
Photo courtesy of Sue Wardlaw Wantland

In the trunk with these documents was a letter my mom had written Mrs. Haworth in November of 1946 asking for some advice. I was about nine years old and asking questions about being adopted. Mrs. Haworth responded with the following letter with sage advice.

> Dear Mrs. Ingle:
>
> I was glad to hear from you concerning your little girl. I know it is a worry to understand how to approach a child relative to her questions. Tell her that her mother was not in position to keep her as she had to work to make a living and you came up here and chose her out of a group of babies for your very own. Tell her she is a "chosen" child. Some foster mothers make a study of things like this and have their own little stories to tell their children. We have always been so busy placing the babies and with each circumstance being different, we have never made a study of explaining these things ourselves.
>
> My daughter Ruth says Sue is full of questions and she probably will always be that way about everything. She will make a good business woman someday. A mother has to be right on her toes and ready for emergencies when her children come to her with outlandish questions. As the little girl grows older, these things will work out themselves. Girls are different from boys, anyway, in that respect. Cleo will enjoy Don's company now from time to time when they go on hunting trips and the like, and as your little Sue grows older you will enjoy her companionship, also. I never get tired of my children. Guess you are seeing Ruth and the children this time as they are in Tulsa now. I am glad you wrote me and wish I could be of more service to you, but you know best how to handle those children as you are better acquainted with them than I am. I would never tell a child the mother died.

MANSION ON A HILL

I am enclosing the parental records of both children, which of course, is the same information which was given to you when you came here for the babies. There is no further information to be had as we have had no communication from either of the mothers since they left here.

Trusting this information will be of some assistance to you in determining what course to follow with Sue and the kindest regards to all of your, I am

Most sincerely,

Cora M. Haworth

I guess I was always interested in knowing more about my birth mother from the time I was little. It is the need to know "who" and "why" that so many adoptees have. My brother had no interest at all in knowing about his birth mother. He wouldn't even admit that he was adopted until right before he passed away, so he never did any searching. I never wanted to hurt my parents' feelings or offend them. I never really asked much or did any searching for my birth parents while they were alive.

However, in 1958 when I was pregnant with my own daughter, I wrote to The Willows and asked for any information they could give to me about my descendants and medical background. I got a letter back from a Garnet Haworth, the daughter-in-law of Cora Haworth, who took over running The Willows. Mrs. Haworth wrote this letter:

Jan. 4, 1958

Dear Mrs. DeWees:

KELLEE PARR

Relative to your recent letter asking for information concerning your natural parents, we are giving you herewith such information as we have available in our files:

Mother: Age 20, weight 136 pounds, height 5 ft. 5 in.
Blond curly hair, hazel eyes
High school graduate, a year of nurses' training.
Student nurse.
Member of Baptist church.
Extraction, English
Ancestral health, no hereditary diseases, no T. B.
Siblings, brother in high school, sister in kindergarten work
Patient's father was a chemist

Father: Age 23 years, weight 165 pounds, height 5 ft. 8 in.
Red curly hair, brown eyes
High school graduate, an office worker.
Church connection, unknown
Extraction, English
Ancestral health, no hereditary diseases, no T. B.
An only child.
Father a merchant.

Birthdate: July 17, 1937, normal delivery, hour, 5:20 p.m. weight 7-1oz.

Trusting this is the information you desired and with our best wishes for your coming motherhood, I am

Very truly yours,

Garnet Haworth

PIONEERS IN THIS SPECIALIZED ETHICAL SERVICE

At one time I lived in San Francisco for seven years. I did have one experience when I was there that really caught me off guard. A lady walked up to me that I had never seen before and said, "You must be one of the Wardlaws."

I was taken aback and said, "What?"

She said, "You must be one of the Wardlaws, you look just like them."

She was a vacationer from South Carolina and had just randomly stopped to tell me that in the street. I didn't know what to say and then she was gone. I knew my birth name was Esther Wardlaw, but I was too startled and didn't think to get any more information from her. Of course, I never saw her again but would forever remember that experience.

My parents passed away in the 70s. It wasn't until after they passed away that I did any searching for my birth parents. I figured searching for the last name Wardlaw wouldn't be too bad because there aren't many Wardlaws. I looked and looked but never had any luck until I finally I contacted the Jackson County Courthouse in Kansas City. I talked to a lady in the office, and even with the possibility of losing her job, she asked me to guess which state my birth mother was from. When I said South Carolina, she said, "That was right."

That was confirmation from what my dad had told me. At least I had it narrowed down to one state out of fifty. The county office couldn't give me any more information, but they said they had two people who I could employ to help me look. These search agents could use their information to search for my birth mother but couldn't share it with me even if they found my birth mother. They could notify the birth mother or family that I was looking for but that was all. So, I hired one of these ladies in March of 2008. She soon wrote to me and said:

> Someone is doing genealogy on the Wardlaw family from the state we spoke of. I wouldn't be able to give you any identifying information unless the courts approve. If we locate the birth

mother and she signs a consent form, then I could release her name and address.

I was excited that we might be making some progress. This search agent kept in touch and in April she found one of my cousins.

I spoke with the daughter to your birth mother's brother mentioned in your family history that you have. She knew of your birth mother. She told me that your birth mother did finish her nurses training, and in fact, became an operating room nurse. There she met and married an ear, nose and throat doctor. They had one son. She quit working to be a stay at home mom. Unfortunately, your birth mother passed away at the age of 53.

The census was available for the year I was born. I searched for the name Wardlaw. This helped me a lot, along with information I got from Ancestry.com. We figured out my birth mother's first name was Helen. (Interesting that my adopted mother's name was Helene.) I also located the cousin who the search agent had contacted. Her name was Dottie and lived in Greensboro, North Carolina. I found my cousin's contact information and gave her a call. She was so funny when I called. I had asked her if there had been any rumors about my mother. She said, "Well, I heard there had been like five miscarriages. Eventually she carried a baby nine months and had a son."

That meant I had another brother ten years younger than me. I asked Dottie if there were any other rumors. She hesitated and said that there had been a rumor of an earlier baby. I laughed and said, "Well, I'm that rumor."

Dottie's response was, "Come see me!"

This was April 9, 2008, and Dottie and I emailed back and forth. Dottie wrote:

MANSION ON A HILL

Sue, I am so pleased to know about you as well. I'll look forward to your visit and will try to prepare in my head the "Wardlaw history" that I know. You and your daughter are very welcome to stay in our home. We will just relax and chat about how wonderful the world can really be. I'm truly looking forward to knowing you and your family and will try to be helpful to you as you discover your birth family. Stay safe and let me know what your plans are. Stay in touch and welcome.

Within weeks my daughter and I flew to Greensboro to meet my cousin. She was absolutely wonderful. It was so strange. Dottie said the minute she saw me she knew who I was. Apparently, I do look just like my mother. Guess the lady who saw me in San Francisco was right. Dottie was very close to my mother, and she said seeing me was just like looking at Aunt Helen. Our connection was overwhelming. It made me realize the strength of being blood relatives. It was something I had never experienced.

Cousins, Dottie in front and Sue in back

Photo courtesy of Sue Wardlaw Wantland

Dottie gave me photos of my mother, a frame of documents for the DAR (Daughter of the American Revolution), and her dance pin. Dottie's father (my mother's brother) had just passed away or he could have probably shared my birth father's name, but Dottie had no idea who he might be. Sadly, my brother had already passed away as well so I never got to meet him. —he only one left of my mother's family is Dottie, her daughter, and a nephew, (my brother's son). —hey are just wonder-ful people.

Helen Wardlaw Morton, Sue's biological mother
Photo courtesy of Sue Wardlaw Wantland

Dottie took me to Salem where my mother is buried. I found out she was born in Arkansas when her father was working there, but they lived in North Carolina when she passed away in 1970. It was so fascinating to learn about my mother and her life. I know my birth mother went to The Willows with her mother, but I don't know if they went by train or car.

Since learning about my birth mother, there are so many coincidences I find quite interesting. My birth mother was twenty when she had me. I gave birth to my daughter when I was twenty years old. After having my daughter, I had several miscarriages the same as my birth mother. My birth mother had a hormonal imbalance, and she went to Philadelphia to a hospital where she stayed during her pregnancy until she had my brother. My birth mother was a nurse, and my daughter became a nurse. My daughter loved finding out her grandmother had the same passion for nursing, and maybe that is where she got her passion.

Sue Ingle (Esther Wardlaw) Wantland in 2017
Photo courtesy of Sue Wardlaw Wantland

Chapter 16

Carol's Story
(1944)

If there is another person with more connection to The Willows than Carol Haworth Price, I don't know who it would be. She also was born at The Willows and was adopted into the Haworth family. I have enjoyed getting to know her and learn more about her family and The Willows. She has great memories growing up in the Haworth family and visiting The Willows when her grandparents and mother operated it. She has become a great friend, and I appreciate what her family did many years ago to help my family.

Carol was born at The Willows on March 23, 1944. Her parents, Don and Garnet "Peggy" Haworth had no children together, though Don had a son from a previous marriage. The couple talked to Don's parents E.P. and Cora May Haworth, who operated The Willows, about adopting a baby. Cora thought it was a great idea and said she would find the perfect baby for them. At first they had talked about wanting to adopt a baby boy, but when they saw Carol, they knew she was their baby. She was a blue-eyed, blond-haired, beautiful baby. Her parents were so thrilled to bring her into their family. "I wouldn't have traded my parents for anything in the world," Carol said. "I am so very, very grateful that there was someone who felt the need to give her child up for adoption so that my mother and father could have a child."

Two-month-old Carol in 1944
Photo courtesy of Carol Haworth Price

Peggy, flower girl Carol, and Don in 1948
Photo courtesy of Carol Haworth Price

The Haworth home was a wonderful place to grow up. Her parents provided Carol a great life, and she will forever be thankful for her upbringing. She always knew she was adopted, and her parents made sure she understood that she was chosen, making her always feel very special. "Mother and Dad started telling me about being adopted as soon as possible," Carol said. "When I was a year old and could listen to stories, they began reading a book to me called, *The Chosen Baby* by Valentina P. Wasson. It is a happy story of adoption."

***The Chosen Baby* originally published in 1939**
Photo courtesy of Carol Haworth Price

She remembers one day her mom got a call from Carol's third grade teacher asking, "What's the deal? Is it true that Carol was adopted?"

The teacher informed Mrs. Haworth that Carol had been telling everybody she was adopted and had been "chosen." The other children became jealous, wanting to be adopted, too. Her mom told the teacher it was true that Carol was adopted, and she was chosen to be a part of their family. Carol has always been open about the fact that she was adopted. Many friends and people she has met over the years have come to her to talk about being adopted themselves.

MANSION ON A HILL

One incident involving her being adopted had a huge impact on Carol's life. She had a boyfriend, and they had talked about getting married. When he found out she was adopted, he told her he couldn't marry her. He wanted to go into politics and felt it would damage his reputation if he married someone who was adopted. Carol was devastated. Later in life, this person came to her and apologized. He said he was embarrassed that he had been so naive and stupid. Her response was, "Yes, you were. I have to agree with you on that one."

Her parents never said too much about her birth parents, but she was given a piece of paper with a little information about her birth mother. She was twenty-two years old. She was a piano player and quite short at five feet four. Carol being much taller figures her birth father must have been tall. It also said her birth mother had wavy hair. Carol laughed, "I have nothing but perfectly straight hair. Guess I didn't get that gene either. I had to start getting perms when I was five years old to get curls."

Carol never felt the need to find her birth parents. "That is something I think has made me who I am," Carol said. "I had such a close and secure feeling of love from my mom and dad that I never have felt anything other than they are my parents. They are the ones who changed my diapers, cleaned up when I was sick, sat by my side when I was hurting, and raised me to give of myself to others if I could do something to make a difference. No one else could take their place. I have never had any feeling of loss by not knowing the person that gave birth to me. I am very grateful to her that she chose to give me life. I have had a wonderful life, and I plan to keep it going!"

Carol went on to say, "My mom was always very open about my birth mother. She told me any number of times if I wanted to meet her or wanted information she was able to do that. As she got older, she would tell me if I wanted info, I was running out of time for her help. Always told her no. To be fair, I always knew my birth mother's name and the name she had given me. Although my card in the book of ba-

KELLEE PARR

bies born at The Willows was removed many years ago, I have the info from my mom. My birth certificate has Garnet and Donald Haworth as my parents, and that's the way I want it to stay."

Carol remembers spending a lot of time at The Willows as a little girl. Most weekends she would go with her parents to visit her grandparents. Sunday dinner was for the entire family to get together. Her grandmother had an apartment at The Willows and lived there all the time. For Sunday dinners, her grandmother had a small private dining room close to the kitchen, separate from the main dining room where the girls dined. The Willows' cook, who actually lived at the maternity home, prepared the meals for them as well as for the girls.

Her grandparents also had a house that was their family home and her grandfather stayed there, not at The Willows. They had three children, Don, Ruth Alice, and Lucille. Carol said, "Lucille was only thirty-four years old when she passed away. She was crippled and had an enlarged heart. She was the most wonderful person with a fabulous sense of humor. I loved her so much. It was very hard for my grandmother to care for her and run the hospital, but she did it with help from the nursing staff, too."

Carol read in her baby book that when she was about one year old, her parents had actually moved into The Willows to stay and run it while Cora went on an extended trip to a conference. Her dad had written in her book how exhausted they were from all the work it took to keep things going on a daily basis and wondered how his mother did it.

E.P. and Cora were very loving people. Carol's grandparents felt a strong passion for their mission to assist young women who needed their help. They were both well-educated and well-read. Her grandfather graduated from Earlham College in Richmond, Indiana, a Quaker college. "My granddad was a strikingly handsome man, tall and slender with beautiful white hair," Carol said. "He always walked with a world-class walking cane. He was a very soft-spoken man always looked very distinguished."

MANSION ON A HILL

Carol's Granddad E. P. Haworth in 1954
Photo courtesy of Carol Haworth Price

Her grandfather loved reading and writing poetry. After he was no longer involved in The Willows, he began writing poetry and published a couple of books: *Sunshine and Roses* and M*akin' Rhymes and Other Rhymes*. Carol still has all of his poetry books.

Poetry books by Edwin P. Haworth
Photos courtesy of Carol Haworth Price

He was also a philatelist, one who collects or studies stamps. He had an extensive stamp collection that included first day issues. That collection was given to Earlham College at his death. Carol shared, "A funny story about my grandfather at the time of his death that I can't forget. The family members were gathered to speak with the minister that would do his service. As I was introduced, the minister stated, 'You look more like a Haworth than anyone else!' It got a chuckle from everyone. Of course, he had no idea I was adopted."

Carol adored her grandmother. "She was a wonderful lady! And a lady she was," Carol said. "She was so good to me. I saw her frequently and especially at our Sunday dinners in her private dining room. She collected plates of many genres and had them all hung on the walls of her dining room. I remember loving to look at them. One in particular always stuck with me of General Dwight Eisenhower. She had several books on him and actually knitted him a scarf. Needless to say, she thought highly of the President to be!"

"She was my 'Baba' and taught me to embroider and knit!" Carol shared. "I loved her so much and truly missed her when she passed away. She passed away at the age of seventy-seven on Christmas morning in her apartment at The Willows. I was only nine years old but had already learned so much from her."

MANSION ON A HILL

Carol's Grandmother "Baba" and Granddad Haworth
Photo courtesy of Carol Haworth Price

In addition to her many duties with The Willows, Cora was active in the community. But more than anything, she loved her girls and the work she did in helping them. The very first girl they took in was the daughter of a friend. The family was a very upstanding family, and they were devastated that the young girl had gotten pregnant. They were going to send her off to live with distant relatives, but Cora told them they should have the girl come live with her. She would help to find an adoptive family for the baby. This started a family mission that lasted sixty-four years.

One of Carol's earliest memories of The Willows was getting in trouble one day while visiting. In the foyer there was a large console table with a huge mirror. On the table sat a beautiful music box that Carol loved. The music box, about three feet in length, was made from inlaid wood pieces. A Swiss-made Sublime Harmonie Music Box, it was patented in the United States in 1875. Inside the lid there was a little piece of paper that listed the twelve songs it would play. One day she opened the music box. For some unknown reason, she felt the need to tear off the paper. Carol said she got in huge trouble over that one. After her mother passed away, Carol was able to keep the music box and still has it on display in her home.

Carol and The Willows' music box

When Carol was in fourth grade, her grandmother passed away. Carol's mother took over running The Willows with no qualms at all about taking over the operations from her mother-in-law. Garnet believed in The Willows and bought it from Cora May's estate. It was an honor in her eyes to continue the mission her in-laws had started so many years earlier. The transition went fairly smoothly as the staff and nurses stayed on and helped Garnet to run the facility. While Carol's grandmother had an apartment in The Willows, her mother never lived there. Carol didn't ever work at The Willows but from time to time, when visiting her mother, would help feed the babies. She loved how devoted her mother was to helping the girls. Garnet ran The Willows for another sixteen years until its closing in 1969.

"My mother lived and breathed the home," Carol said. "It was a 24-hour-a-day job. If a girl was flying in to the airport at 1 a.m., Mother would go to the airport and meet her. It was amazing to watch Mother when someone was in labor. You would think all the girls were her own; she paced the floor just like any parent."

Garnet "Peggy" Haworth
Photo courtesy of Carol Haworth Price

One of the amazing aspects of The Willows was that so many of the staff worked there for almost their entire careers. Mrs. Maudene Lowe began her career at The Willows in around 1913 as a stenographer. She became the business secretary and was associated with the homes administration staff for fifty-three years. Mrs. Alice Dysart was superintendent of nurses. She trained nurses and oversaw patients and babies for thirty years. Carol said, "She retired and then when Mom was going to close The Willows, she came back to help her."

Carol kept an article from *The Kansas City Star* dated July 15, 1969, when The Willows was closing. The article talks about both Mrs. Dysart and Mrs. Lowe and their thoughts about their times at The Willows:

> Mrs. Alice U Dysart, whose job the last 30 years as superintendent of nurses and overseeing patients and babies, remembers everyone seemed to want to adopt "blond, blue-eyed babies."
>
> "We would match up the background of the babies with that of the new parents," she said, "and bring out about two or three infants for the couple to see. We would silently pick out one we thought was best for them and show them that baby first; then the others. They would almost always decide on the first one.
>
> "The personal happiness I've gained from working here is a great satisfaction to me. Some girls have come in so vindictive. When you know you've done something to help them in mind and spirit, it makes you feel good. And when you see new parents leaving the home hand in hand, it's an unforgettable sight.
>
> "There have been many dramas through the years. One girl was told by a doctor that she wouldn't survive childbirth and she had given away all her clothes when she came. Of course, she lived. Another came in with a crippled hip, which the doctors mended after her baby was born."
>
> Mrs. Lowe, who has been with the home since "Don Haworth was in knee pants with buckles," said that if the girls cried when they came into The Willows, they cried even harder when they left.

Another longtime employee was Mrs. Nellie McEwen. She was head of adoption for forty-eight years. She was at The Willows when

Leona arrived way back in 1925. Carol doesn't know why, but Mrs. McEwen always terrified her. She was never anything but nice to Carol, but maybe it was her no-nonsense personality. She was very thorough and efficient, the perfect administrator to oversee the massive number of adoptions. The majority of letters received by adoptive parents from The Willows were from Mrs. McEwen.

Joan Nichols was the social worker at The Willows for ten years. She was an employee of the Jackson County Juvenile Court. She worked with other maternity facilities, but most of her cases were with girls from The Willows. Because she spent a large amount of time at The Willows when not at court, Carol's mother provided an office for Mrs. Nichols, where she met with the girls and adoptive parents. Joan and Garnet became very, very close friends, and the families remained close even after The Willows closed. "She was wonderful. There was no kinder person than Mrs. Nichols," Carol said.

First photo: Alice Dysart, Nellie McEwen, and Joan Nichols
Second photo: Maudene Lowe
Photos courtesy of Carol Haworth Price

Mrs. Nichols was quoted in an article in the paper about Peggy (Garnet) after her passing at the age of eight-nine.

> *"She delighted in doing anything for the girls," Nichols said. "If a girl would get a little homesick, she would get up in the middle of the night and come over to comfort her."*

From the very beginning, the Haworths and The Willows' staff always believed in protecting the privacy of the young women they helped through a difficult time. They promised the young women and families they would forever keep their secret. Because of this promise, in the 1980s Carol worked very hard with a friend to keep the adoption records closed in Missouri. She and her friend, who was an adoptive mother, appeared in front of the Missouri State Congress and testified against the Model Adoption Act. The Act proposed changing the procedure for placement of adoptees from licensed child care placing agencies to unlicensed intermediaries. The Act also sought to give access to original birth certificates to adoptees. She felt it was important to continue to provide the privacy of the birth mothers unless they have given permission for their names to be disclosed. "It was not because I was being mean spirited. It was because I believed then – and still do – that a promise is a promise!" Carol said. "Those girls that had been under my family's care were promised their secret would be kept. I felt that should have been enough reason to keep the adoption records closed. I understand that there are many reasons people want the information available to them. I think if both parties, birth mother and adoptee, want to share their information then that should be allowed."

This is Carol's testimony on May 9, 1980:

> I am Carol Price, a 36-year-old adopted child. My grandparents opened The Willows Maternity Sanitarium for unwed mothers in Kansas City, Missouri in 1905. At my grandmother's death in 1953 my mother took over as superintendent and owner until she closed The Willows in June 1969. As a result of her expertise, my daily contacts with unwed mothers, and the adoption procedures, as well as being adopted myself, I have gained knowledge and insight that the majority of people rarely hear about and never experience firsthand. It is through my experiences, knowledge and personal feelings that I must oppose portions of the Model Adoption Act.
>
> First, I am concerned about the standards for the placement of children by unlicensed intermediaries, which are less stringent than those of licensed child placing agencies. If this legislation is truly for the benefit of the child, as it is supposed to be, then there should be uniform standards for all involved in the placement of a child. As now written, the double standards will only facilitate the black-market placement of infants. It will do nothing beneficial for the hard to place child. What is

more important – to get a child placed in a family, or, to get a child placed in a family that is the best one for him? Only under equal conditions can the child have the assurance of being placed in the proper home, with the proper adoptive parents.

Secondly, the recommendation to open birth records to adult adoptees has extremely serious implications. In most states the age of majority is 18, but as a teenager, an 18-year-old is still struggling with his identity and his independence. He is still seeking to find his way in our society. How easy it would be for an adopted 18-year-old when still in conflict between himself and his adoptive parents to seek out his birth parents as a false solution to his conflicts. The damage he could do to himself, his adoptive family, and his birth parents is devastating and irreversible.

I am not saying that in some instances this cannot be a good experience for I believe it can. I am only stating that under no circumstances should there be open birth records. Any seeking out of birth parents or adopted children should be done through the court acting as intermediary. It should always be, and without question, the right of either the adoptee or the birth parents to deny any request. Anything less than equal rights for the child, the birth parents and the adoptive parents is completely against all of the principals this country has struggled for since its beginning. To take rights from one and give to another is not only unfair but is unjust.

Carol is proud of her family heritage. The Haworths played a big part in Kansas City being known as the "Adoption Hub of America." "I think it was a very important part of Kansas City, and it drew a lot of people to Kansas City," Carol said. "It was just part of the wonderful warmness the people in Kansas City have."

MANSION ON A HILL

**Three generations of Haworth men
E.P., Donald, and David, Carol's brother**
Photo courtesy of Carol Haworth Price

She knows how many lives her family touched. Her grandparents and parents genuinely cared for the young women who faced such trying times. Providing seclusion and anonymity for girls in trouble, The Willows allowed the young women to return home to lives without society's condemnation. Babies born out of wedlock were found homes with adoptive parents desperately wanting to start families.

The success of The Willow's mission in providing privacy is apparent in the fact that so few today are aware of its history. The hundreds of thousands of lives touched by The Willows include the young women who were residents, the babies given up for adoption, the adoptive couples blessed with a child, and all the family relationships that followed. Having been a Willow's baby herself, Carol feels fortunate to be raised by such a loving family. She is forever grateful to her grandparents for having the heart and foresight to start The Willows over a century ago.

Peggy and Don at Carol's wedding, Nov. 17, 1973
Carol and husband, Bud, at vows renewal, Dec. 1, 2017
Photos courtesy of Carol Haworth Price

Chapter 17

Anita's Story
(1949)

It has been a pleasure to get to know Anita. I was so excited when she contacted me and asked if she could share her story. Hers is unique in that she returned to The Willows to visit the place of her birth. Her vivid memory and her experience gave me goosebumps when I read it.

I was born at The Willows in 1949. My folks did not hide the fact that I was adopted and always knowing was a good thing for me. This life would never have happened except that my mother had me at The Willows, and I was adopted by my wonderful parents. My life was not that of a normal young girl from the United States. I was raised all over the world as my adoptive dad was an archaeologist, and I spent most of my growing up years in Arab Palestine. My family came back to the United States when my grandma was sick and a couple other times for Dad's stuff. When in the U.S., we lived in Illinois and later, after my mom got sick, in Minnesota.

In 1962, we had just returned from overseas. My mother's mother was ill, and my mother needed to be available to help. We were living in Illinois where my dad was a college professor. My folks talked about the whole struggle to have a baby and then to find one when they could not have one. I have some of my dad's correspondence with The Willows from that time. I also have some of the things they had to file after they took me home. My dad was a camera nut, and he took movies of walking down the steps at The Willows and putting me in the car. I don't know what happened to that movie reel, but I remember seeing it many times.

We had a sort of tradition in our house. You got to ask for one thing for your birthday, and – if it was feasible – you got it. The year I turned thirteen, I told my dad I wanted to go to The Willows and see where I was born. Dad said, "We'll see," which usually meant "No." But I still hoped.

We traveled a lot so being on another trip on my birthday was not a giveaway. It was mid-morning when we pulled up in front of a huge house set back off the sidewalk. Since I had my nose in a book as usual, I had no idea where I was when the car stopped. I only vaguely remember the street. There were lots of trees, and the sidewalk seemed wide. From the eyes of a child, it was quiet and peaceful. Dad said, "This is where you were born."

I was so astonished and amazed my dad had honored my wish. I was giddy with excitement. He continued, "We parked our car about right here when we came to get you."

He asked if I wanted to go inside and of course I excitedly blurted out, "Yes!"

We got out of the car and walked up to the front door. I was pretty excited and anxious. I don't actually remember the walk to the house. The walk itself was not important at the time for my memory. Secretly, I was thinking that my birth mother had walked here once, and I felt a bit guilty about those thoughts. I didn't want my parents to know how I was feeling being so close to where my birth mother had actually been.

We went inside, and my dad went to the office to speak to someone about a tour. I remember sitting in the vestibule with Mom while Dad talked to the lady in the office. It was not a fancy hallway at all, and the lights were dim. It didn't take long before I heard loud voices. My dad was being his very adamant self. My dad was sort of famous in his field

MANSION ON A HILL

and had a way of getting what he wanted. He had nine Ph.D. degrees and spoke seventeen languages, so he could be rather arrogant when crossed. That was the guy who came out of the office, and he stayed in that mode until we left. He was not taking "no" for an answer.

My mom was very nervous. That was not a normal reaction from her. We had been in some pretty crazy border-crossing situations in hostile territories where she had not been flustered at all. So, I remember wondering about her nerves now. We were sitting there and my mom finally said, "I don't think they like that we brought you here. They told us that we should not tell you that you were adopted, but Dad did research and felt it was better if you knew."

I am very glad they told me. I spent my life working for Child Protective Services as a social worker. I have seen some pretty devastating things happen when these things are kept secret. I too have adopted and was very open with my daughter about how she came to be part of our family.

Dad and a tall, older woman came out of the office. She was not at all happy. My memory of her was of a disapproving attitude and stiff body language. She seemed tall (to me as a child) and slender with a longer, bob haircut. Her hair was wavy. She was wearing a skirt and blouse, I think. She said that she would give me a brief tour, but I would not see any of the "girls." I nodded, and she told my parents to have a seat.

The first room we went into was a sitting room with sofas and chairs around. There were no lights on. This lady wouldn't turn any on to give me a better look at the room. We went to a room with nicely made beds. It was so tidy I doubt if anyone was using them. Again, no lights were used to show this room. We went to some of the rooms where the babies were kept. After a couple of rooms, we went to a room that was brighter as it had windows that let in light. There were five or six white cribs in this room. I was caught by surprise when a window in the room looked like a window I had had in many of my dreams.

The crib across the room from the small window I would bet had been mine. That window just rang my bell. I looked around the room, smiled at the lady and asked, "Was this my room? The window looks familiar."
    I was so excited in seeing this room. My heart pounded. This poor lady turned white and practically raced back to my parents. She looked at my dad and chided, "I told you this was a bad idea."
    She stalked off to the office and shut the door. Clearly our visit was over. I looked at my parents and shrugged my shoulders but still feeling excitement from the vision of the window in my head.
    We returned to the car, and Dad asked what happened. I told him about the whole tour and the window. I asked him if what I did was wrong because that lady was clearly upset. He said no and guessed that no one expected the babies to be able to remember their time there. To this day that window is a fond memory. I am not sure why. I was only about six months old when I left The Willows. While the window was only a dream memory, it has always stuck with me.
    I have wanted to find my birth family all of my life. It took until the law changed that I was able to obtain the court file. By that time, both of my birth parents and siblings had died. I was very lucky to find nephews. They have been wonderful and accepting of the aunt they never knew they had.
    Thank you for letting me share my story.

Photo of Anita's biological mom that her nephew shared with her
Photo courtesy of Anita Wilhelmi

Chapter 18

Phil's Story
(1950)

After My Little Valentine *was published, my sister shared the book with a family friend, Chuck. He grew up in Kansas City with his best friend, Phil, who was adopted at The Willows. Chuck knew Phil had a wonderful reunion story to share and connected me with Phil. I am sure his story will warm your heart as it did mine.*

I was born March 8, 1950, at The Willows in Kansas City, Missouri. I grew up in Lee Summit, Missouri. My parents brought me home from The Willows on March 17, St. Patrick's Day, so I was blessed to always celebrate two birthdays. It took almost an entire year for the adoption to be finalized. My adoption papers were signed with my adoptive name of Philip Myers sometime around January of 1951. My parents told me when I was little that I was adopted and that I was born at the Children's Hospital in Kansas City. But after I started looking through papers for information about my birth mother, I found out she had been at The Willows, a very famous unwed mothers' home.

Knowing that I was adopted, I never really thought that much about looking for my biological parents, but of course, I was always curious about whether or not I had other brothers or sisters. My adoptive mother shared some of the information she had been told and wrote down when they adopted me. It turned out only part of the information was accurate. My mother's notes said my birth mother was from Texas, a teacher, had been in the Catholic church, and it was from an affair that I had resulted. In actuality, it was the Methodist Church, and she had worked in the administrative offices for a school district in Texas. She had never been married, but it turned out that she had an affair with her long ago high school boyfriend who was already married but had no children. They had a little afternoon tryst and here I am.

When my birth mother became pregnant, she was thirty-nine years old. I figured out her age when I discovered she was born in 1910. What a scandal for a single woman of her age (presumably an old maid in those days) to be pregnant. Her going to The Willows would have been quite different from the majority who went there as teenagers or in their early twenties. How odd it must have been to have been old enough to be some of these girls' mother and to interact with them daily.

In 1992 after my dad passed away, my mother gave me all my adoption papers. After going through them, I discovered my biological mom had given me a name. On the papers, it said I was Gerard Callahan. I am a little bit Irish, I think. Once my adoptive mom passed, I went back to Lee Summit for a class reunion in about 1998. While I was there, I went to the Jackson County Courthouse and checked the adoption records. They gave me information to fill out and instructions to send some money. They also said I had to include a letter with permission from my adoptive parents to look for my birth mother or copies of death certificates of the adoptive parents. Since my parents had both passed, I got copies of their death certificates, filled out the form and sent in the money.

Several weeks went by and the staff at the courthouse sent me the non-disclosure information they had. How excited I was to get the nine- or ten-page typed narrative that my biological mother had given to them, something she had written herself. All the identifying information, such as her name, where she came from, and other demographics had been blacked out. But knowing she was thirty-nine years old, it made sense for her to write such a long narrative because she had lived quite a life already compared to the young girls just starting out in life. Some of her family history was included. Of course, no names, but it did tell me that she lived in a town of 200,000 people.

The Jackson County Court also gave me a list of court-approved search agents. These are people who can use the court's information to try and find biological parents. When the search agent has any luck, he or she asks the birth parents if they are interested in contacting the searching child. The search agent cannot divulge information to the child and has to protect the biological parents' rights if they do not want to be found.

Looking over the list, I picked a lady's name I liked. I think she was from Minnesota. So, I contacted her and found she asked a slight fee to help with the search. I hired her and the adventure continued. This search agent had the actual name and contact information for my biological mom. She tried to call and couldn't get anyone to answer.

My wife Charleen and I would talk to this search agent on the phone, but she couldn't tell us much. Instead, she would give clues. Turned out one of the phone numbers the search agent was trying to reach was one of my birth mother's cousins. She said, "Well, she is still alive, but they had to put her into a nursing home. Her only sister had passed away, and she couldn't take care of herself."

One day I was talking on the phone with this search agent and I was sharing the information my birth mother had written about living in a city with a population of about 200,000 in the 1940s. The first city that came to mind that was close to Kansas City was Omaha, Nebraska. I said to the lady, "I know you can't tell me where, but Omaha is..." and she interrupted me and said, "It isn't that far away."

I remembered the notes my adoptive mom had written when I was adopted. They said the birth mother was from Texas. At that time, I was living in Bryan, Texas, outside College Station, working at Texas

A&M. I got to thinking about larger cities in Texas that might have had that size population in the 1940s. I narrowed the list down to Houston, Austin, Dallas, Ft. Worth, El Paso, and San Antonio. My wife and I were again on the phone talking to the search agent. We started mentioning cities that probably **would not** be right. "El Paso was an outlier and seemed too far out."

"Probably so," she would acknowledge.

We went through the rest of the list of cities the same way. Always "probably so" and not the right city. Then my wife said to me, "You didn't mention San Antonio."

The search agent said, "I didn't say that."

We knew without her saying.

Through my birth mother's narrative, I realized this woman had never married. Callahan had to be her real last name. It also said in the narrative that she was very big in the Women's Guild of the Methodist Church. That was part of the shame, too I guess, for her being unwed and being a mother. I spent quite a bit of time in San Antonio doing trainings so one time I got a San Antonio phone book while I was there. One day Charleen picked up the phone book and turned to the yellow pages. She began calling the Methodist churches listed. She would ask the person that answered if they knew of or had a woman in the Women's Guild with the last name Callahan. The seventh church, now that is divine isn't it, had a woman answer the phone. When asked if she knew a lady with last name Callahan she said, "Oh yes, Callahan, oh you mean Beatrice. Her sister Evelyn just passed away."

Okay! I had her first name, Beatrice. A little bit of irony, her middle name is Virginia and my adoptive mother's first name was Virginia. This is all divine in my mind. I then made contact with the preacher at the church. I first called him telling who I was and why I was calling. Then I wrote a letter and sent it to him. I included a second letter to share with Beatrice asking if she would like to see me and that I would like to meet her. I said there were no hard feelings. I didn't blame her for anything. I have a good life and would like to meet her. The preacher went to see Beatrice in the nursing home and her first reaction was, "No, let's leave the past in the past."

I sort of brushed it off and figured maybe I don't want to meet her either. One never knows what you might find and must be prepared for what's there rather than have preconceived ideas. It might not be as good as you think.

Charleen pushed me to keep pursuing. We went to San Antonio to the church and visited with the preacher. We went to the service and listened to his sermon. After church, we sat down with the preacher and his wife. We told them we would like to go see Beatrice. He said no, he didn't think we would want to go see her, but the preacher's wife emphatically said, "Yes, go do it."

My wife, bless her heart, is the aggressive one here. She's the risk taker. She took the bulletin from the church service, and we drove over to the nursing home. She went in first alone. She said she was from the church and would like to see Beatrice. I had my youngest child with me, and we drove around the block, waiting for her to call me to see how things went. After Charleen met Beatrice, she chatted with her for a little bit, eventually telling the older woman that she was her son's wife. She showed her baby pictures of me and asked Beatrice if she would like to meet me. Of course, with the evidence right there in front of her, Beatrice just couldn't say no.

Charleen called me, and I went to see my birth mother for the first time. Now without doubt, I know who I look like. It was so interesting to learn the story of how she got to The Willows. After her little encounter and she realized she was pregnant, she went to the family doctor. Because she was an unwed mother, it had to be kept quiet. They brought in the biological father, the doctor, and the doctor's wife. They were the only four who knew her secret and that I even existed. The father couldn't get a divorce and was scared to death of his wife finding out. He said he would help to pay to get her to The Willows. She got on the train in San Antonio, Texas, and went to The Willows. Beatrice's parents had already passed, and there was only her sister Evelyn. The doctor told everyone she had a tumor and had to go to Kansas City to get treatment. I still chuckle that I was a tumor. So somewhere around October of 1949 she was on a train headed to Kansas City and not long after March 8 she was on a train back home. I asked her if that was a lonely ride back home and she said, "Yeah, it was."

My father's family never knew about me. He lived in a town not too far from San Antonio, and he passed away in the 1980s. He never had any children, and I never met any of his family.

**Phil's biological parents, Beatrice and her love William Mills
17 years of age**
Photo courtesy of Philip Myers

I had four or five dinners with Beatrice before she passed away in 2002 and got to know her well. It was quite an adventure searching for her, and I was very happy to get to know her. I had been told Beatrice was a school teacher, but she actually worked in the administrative office in the San Antonio School District. She said birthdays and holidays were always hard for her. She always wondered where I was and what had happened to me. Thankfully during the times we got together, I could fill in the gaps for her.

Beatrice told me that she had always lived in the same house her father built in 1906. It was getting in bad shape by the time she had to move out. The state was about to make her a ward, but her niece stepped in. A nice lady in a private nursing home agreed to take her in so she wouldn't get thrown into the state adult disability system. Beatrice lived a very long life, and she got to meet her kid and her grandkids.

Beatrice and her older sister, Evelyn
Photo courtesy of Philip Myers

One of the coolest parts to my story is the minute that Beatrice saw me and admitted that I existed, she wasn't an angry, grumpy old woman any more. It was like you could see the weight of guilt lifted off her. I felt it was truly a blessing to know we had done that for her.

MANSION ON A HILL

Phil, Beatrice and Phil's youngest son, Brady taken in 1998
Photo courtesy of Philip Myers

Chapter 19

Jill's Story
(1950s)

Jill and I met on Facebook through The Willows Maternity Group. She posted about having a special reunion with her biological parents. I wrote to her and asked if she would like to share her story in my book. So happy she said yes. We chatted on the phone for a couple hours. I laughed, cried, and knew this was a very special story that others needed to hear. Anyone questioning if they should look for their biological parent or not need only read about Jill's experience to know it is worth taking the risk. I hope you enjoy her story as much as I have.

Jill was born at The Willows Maternity Hospital in the spring, during the 1950s. When she was growing up, she always believed that all the beautiful flowers were celebrating her birthday. Her adoptive parents lived in Oklahoma. Her mother had two late-term miscarriages. Doctors said that she couldn't carry a baby full term and suggested adoption. They decided to adopt in Missouri because the state had the toughest laws in the nation sealing the adoption records. They were impressed by The Willows' reputation, and the girls that went there, so they chose to work with them. They were thrilled when The Willows called them to pick up a little girl, driving all night so they could be there first thing in the morning. Jill was told this story all her life, just as others are told their birth story. It was obvious that her parents believed that Jill was a gift given in love by a young girl who wanted her to have a good life. From her earliest memories, she knew she was adopted. They told her she was chosen, twice loved, and God had made them a family. Two years later, they returned to The Willows to pick up her little sister.

In today's age, it is very important to know one's medical history. Jill said, "I believe the first thing an adoptee needs to know and a safe thing to ask when searching for birth parents is medical history. Anything on top of that is just gravy. It was always a stickler for me not having the medical history when I went to the doctor. One time a doctor asked me about my history, and I told him I was adopted. He put a big red "X" over the medical history page and I was so offended. It was as if I was a nonperson. When I finally did get my medical history, it was a very exciting thing for me to go to the doctor's office and fill in that missing information for the very first time."

Jill's story in finding her birth mother is a unique one. "I always wanted to find my birth mother," she said. "Throughout my life, stories played in my head about my birth parents. I placed them as high school sweethearts. My parents told me they were too young to have a family, and this made total sense to me. I never felt abandoned like some adoptees do. My birth name was Melanie, and I knew in the bottom of my heart that I was named after Melanie from *Gone with the Wind*. I also knew that my birth mother needed to know the rest of the story. She absolutely needed to know what happened to her baby girl."

These thoughts were always with Jill but not as an obsession. It was more like having curly hair – it was just always there. During her late 40s, her family went through a very rough time. "My dad suffered a horrible stroke, a very close cousin was diagnosed with brain cancer, and my mom developed Alzheimer's disease. Just one devastating thing after another."

They all passed away within five years, her mom dying the day before her 50th birthday. "It was such a difficult time," Jill said. "Sometimes there are things that happen to us in our lives that our family calls blessings in disguise. Where one would say, 'Well, it's not something I would wish for, but this wouldn't have happened if we didn't have this happen or that happen.' My family was searching for blessings in disguise throughout these hard years. After this time, I told my cousin's husband, 'I want a blessing that looks like a blessing. I don't want to look for it. I don't want to hunt it out. I don't want to analyze it. I want an obvious blessing.'"

Six months later, Jill got her blessing that looked like a blessing – and it was a thunderbolt!

After her mom died, she decided to do some adoption searching again. She found the website adoption.com and registered on their free registry. One could place his or her information on the site, stating the desire to search for a birth parent or a child given up for adoption. "On the Registry, I put down that I was a girl born at The Willows and my birthday," Jill said. "I didn't put down my birth name on my adoption papers. I never had much hope this would lead to anything and quickly forgot I had posted the information. Little did I know a guardian angel would come across this site and change my life," Jill added, "I look at this registration like buying one lottery ticket and then winning the big prize."

The guardian angel was Britt from California. She had gone thru a very rough time. While getting her life back on track, Britt met an older woman at a nonprofit organization. This elderly lady named Liz volunteered and donated money to this facility. Britt worked as a case worker there. Liz took Britt under her wing to help her get her life back together. Liz had helped three or four other girls older than Britt over the years and developed close friendships. They just loved one another as family. After celebrating Liz's 69th birthday in December, Britt decided she wanted to give Liz a special present for her 70th birthday. Liz had shared over the years about giving up a baby girl for adoption who had died at the age of sixteen. Britt asked how she knew she had died, and Liz said she just knew. Britt decided she wanted to find out what had happened to Liz's baby. That would be her special birthday present.

Britt started searching in December right after Liz's birthday, which was about seven months after Jill registered at adoption.com in May. After Internet searching for close to six months, Britt came across Jill's information in the website registry. She was so excited. She still had not told Liz anything at all about her quest because it was a surprise birthday present. She also wanted to confirm before she ever told Liz that she had found her baby. It was right after Memorial Day when she contacted Jill. One of those blind, out of the blue, contact things. Jill received a blind email from adoption.com that said, "I am a friend of your birth mother. I want her only daughter to know what a wonderful person she is. She didn't want to give you away. Her mother made her do it. Britt."

Jill completely freaked out because she had forgotten she had even registered her information. Jill called her sister, also adopted from The Willows, and said, "What do I do? What do I do? What do I do?"

Her sister was just as excited for her, and together they composed a noncommittal letter asking for additional information. It might not be true this was her birth mother. Jill asked Britt for her given name at birth for proof of the match.

Not knowing the birth name, Britt had to tell Liz. Britt was so excited by the news she could barely wait until work the next day. As soon as Liz came in, Britt told her that she needed to sit down. Liz asked her, "Why, what's going on?"

"I have found your daughter," Britt said.

"What? She's dead."

"No, she's not. I got an email from her," Britt said, "and she wants to know what you named her."

In shock, Liz told her the information. Britt wrote Jill back and told her the name. The first name Melanie was right, but the last name wasn't the name on Jill's adoption papers. She zipped an email off to

Britt and said this was not the right last name. Britt then wrote her back and told Jill she thought it was time she took herself out of the loop. She gave Jill Liz's phone number and said she was waiting for her call.

As soon as Jill got the email, she called and the first thing she said was that's not the last name on her adoption papers. The first name is right, but the last name is wrong. Liz said, "There can't be any other name on there! What name is on there?"

Jill told her the name and Liz said, "Oh my God, I didn't even think about that."

The last name on the document wasn't the name she had gone by for most of her life. Her mother had remarried when she was little, and she always went by her stepfather's last name even though she wasn't officially adopted. It was her legal name on the adoption paper. Jill said, "She knew my first name, and I knew what her last name was. That was all the proof we needed. We didn't need any blood tests or DNA test or any of that. We talked over two hours that night because Liz didn't know if she would ever hear from me again."

Liz had more problems than Jill did understanding and accepting their reunion because this was all done for them by Britt without Liz knowing. For Jill, at least she had registered on the website to search. Though she didn't really spend time looking, she had it in the back of her mind. The news totally caught Liz off guard. She wasn't searching because in her mind her daughter was dead, even though she did talk about her daughter. Liz didn't have any siblings so she talked to women friends about her baby, which led Britt to her search. Jill said, "If Liz had known our guardian angel was looking for me, she would have told Britt to not do it because I was dead."

"Thankfully, Britt didn't believe her," Jill continued. "So, it was a total surprise for Liz. For some people that might not have worked, but for us it was perfect. Neither one of us had reached out and interfered in the other's life. It was a divine intervention thing, and all worked out just beautifully."

Jill still keeps in touch with Britt today and Britt will tell people that other than the birth of her daughter, this was the most important thing she ever did in her life. Jill said, "If you read books about searching, it will say, 'You should never do this. You should never do that.' Britt did it all wrong according to the books, but it turned out great for us. So, there is no one way to reunite, though one never knows how people will react to the news."

Once they found each other, Jill was totally surprised that Liz told everyone then. It was no longer a secret – Pandora's Box was open! Jill said, "I would laugh because she would tell me she told even total strangers, 'I had a baby when I was eighteen and had to give her away and we just met. I found my daughter!'"

They first talked when Jill was fifty-one. Liz said that at her 50th high school class reunion held a few years earlier, she told all of her high school friends about having a baby. She said it had been fifty years, and she was just going to acknowledge the elephant in the room because she thought they all knew. Only one of her friends knew about her having a baby because Liz talked to her about it when it happened. There were two girls who had guessed. Nobody else at the reunion had a clue. What Liz's family told everyone was that her mother and Liz went to California to live with Liz's uncle because Liz had a fatal blood disease. They were traveling up and down the coast of California trying to find a cure. Her mother lived in California with her brother during this time, and Liz went to The Willows. Liz told Jill, "When people would say they were coming to California and wanted to stop and see my mom and me, my mom gave the excuse we were traveling up and down the coast from my uncle's house seeing doctors. So, it was better for me to be dying than for me to be pregnant."

Once Jill and Liz got to know each other and started swapping photos, Liz decided to send out a birth announcement to all of her friends. She used two photos of Jill and a photo of Jill's kids to put on the announcement. "I've been seeing other's announcements all my life," she said. "By God, I am sending one out!" She sent it out, adding under the kids' picture, "And I am a grandmother."

That first night, Liz told Jill that she could tell her who Jill's father was, but she needed a little time to process this. Jill figured she would still know where he was because Liz told her they had been high school sweethearts from the same hometown and had gone to class reunions. Jill didn't know if they remained in contact over the years, but it turned out they did.

After a month of talking, Liz, Jill, and Britt met face to face. Jill flew to California and Liz met Jill's airplane with an "It's a girl" balloon. Jill says she will always remember that first hug and the overwhelming feelings that swept over her. After that weekend, Liz contacted Jill's birth father, Bill, in Massachusetts, telling him that she had just spent the weekend with their daughter. He was very receptive and gave Liz all his contact numbers so that Jill could call him. Jill talked to him shortly after Liz broke the news.

When Liz knew she was going to send out the "birth" announcement, she called up Bill and said, "If there is anybody you feel you want to tell yourself back home, you better do it, because I am telling everybody. I am tired of this secrecy, and I'm not going to hide any more. It is going to many of our high school friends."

The story was that Bill and Liz were high school sweethearts and grew up in Iowa. After high school, Liz was going to go to college in Missouri. On her way to college, she started throwing up. Her parents took her to an emergency room and found out that she was pregnant. She was very much in denial up to this point. She thought if she didn't say anything then it wasn't true. They were in a small town close to Kansas City and they called a local minister. He brought pamphlets about The Willows.

MANSION ON A HILL

Liz told Jill they just couldn't get married – they were only eighteen, and they had other plans. She wasn't willing to get married and live a lie, even though her parents wanted her to get married. Bill told Jill later that in his mind, Liz made the decision not to get married but to give up the baby instead. She did it because she knew getting married wasn't what he wanted. She was right, but he would have married her if she had not made that decision. Liz told Jill that she had given Bill his life and that is also the truth. Liz's mom really did want her to go to California to have the baby and stay with her brother, but Liz wanted to stay in the Midwest close to Bill. So, she went to The Willows. That was how Jill ended up being born there and given up for adoption.

Jill's parents corresponded the whole time Liz was at The Willows. Bill remembers the day that Liz's dad called him to tell him that his daughter had been born. He said that both Liz and the baby were fine. Bill asked when he could see Liz, and her dad said "NEVER" and hung up. Bill said that he went up to his college room and cried, it was so overwhelming. They continued to date for about a year and a half afterwards before they broke up. They remained caring friends over the years and saw each at reunions and other events. Liz said that she continued to love "father of child" for decades because that made Melanie a "love child." They did talk sometimes about Melanie and wonder where she was.

Jill was very curious about The Willows. Her adoptive parents gave her a photo of the outside of The Willows taken when they adopted her. She always thought what a huge place. It showed a big stairway up to big front doors. Liz said adoptive parents only used the front door to the grand entranceway. The girls came and went out the back door. Liz was able to tell Jill a little about what it was like to stay at The Willows in the 1950s.

When Liz was there, the girls were allowed to leave The Willows for the day to go out to sightsee, shop, or just unwind. It was much different from the early days of The Willows when visitors were not encouraged and socialization was kept inside the walls. However, Liz said they usually stayed at The Willows, where they felt safe, playing cards and watching TV. If they did venture away, they wore fake wedding bands. One of their favorite places was the Plaza. In fact, Bill and his parents came to visit. They took Liz out to dinner and dancing for Valentine's Day. She remembered it well; said she wore a beautiful pink dress. Jill said, "Since I was born in the spring, I am sure she was as big as a house. I imagine my birth father was horrified to see her."

The girls were encouraged to use aliases and only first names (fake if possible). Liz could never do this and went by her real name. After their "freshman year" at The Willows, she went to college and roomed with a girl that she had met at The Willows. Their diet was watched carefully during their time at The Willows so that after they left, their bodies didn't look like they had just had a baby. Everything done during this time was so that when they left, they could completely forget this time, and no one would ever know. Liz was told by her mother not to tell her secret to anyone – including her husband to be. But she did tell him. Keeping this secret and believing that people knew of it during all those years caused a lot of emotional damage to Liz. One of the amazing things that Liz said was that she and her mother had never discussed Melanie, Liz's only child and her mother's only grandchild.

Liz said that she went into labor while watching "The Mickey Mouse Club." This tidbit seemed appropriate. After Jill was born, Liz was never allowed to touch or hold her baby. Liz told Jill that she asked every single day if she could see her baby, and they wouldn't let her. The girls at The Willows were divided into two sections of the house. One section was for girls who were still pregnant, and the other was for girls who had given birth. After Liz gave birth to Jill and was on this other side of the house, there was a nurse who was very nice to her. At the end of a week of begging to see her baby, this nurse came and got her. They stood up on the stairs where there was a window a person could look out and see the entrance of The Willows. There was a family – a father,

MANSION ON A HILL

a mother and a baby – heading down the stairs to a car. Liz told Jill the nurse had said, "That's your baby. Don't they look like a beautiful family?"

Liz had this image in her head her whole life. She said to Jill, "Anytime I thought about you, I thought about you with that family because I had seen you with your parents. I knew you were going to be okay because I knew this was a beautiful family."

After this nurse had shown Liz the adoptive family, it really did help her since she knew what happened to her little girl. Unfortunately, that wasn't Jill's parents. She told Liz, "That was not my parents. Birth mothers by law had one month to change their minds before the babies could be placed for adoption. Didn't they tell you that you had a month to change your mind?"

She said, "No, what do you mean it wasn't you?"

"My parents didn't get there until I was a month old, and you were already gone," Jill said and asked again, "Didn't they tell you that you had a month?"

"No, they didn't tell me that," she said. "Well, they might have told me. I don't remember anything that the attorney told me when I signed the papers. But there was no way I could take you home."

Jill assured her that she understood and absolutely knew that. The authorities at The Willows told Liz that she could never look for her baby, she had signed away all her rights. She also heard there had been a bonfire at The Willows where the records were burned, so she believed there was no way to even start. She said, "Not only I wouldn't have known how to go about looking for you, but I never would have because I was told I couldn't."

Jill's adoptive mom had to send updates to Kansas City to The Willows every month to tell them how Jill was doing. Her mom kept copies of those for Jill, and she took those for Liz to read so she would know how much her parents really wanted her. Jill said, "It was fine for me to tell her how much my parents loved me, and I was treated just like their own, but it was a whole different thing to see what my mom wrote about those first couple of months. Although she wouldn't read the letters because of the pain it caused, the number of letters meant so much to her to know I had been so loved and wanted."

Liz never had another child. She told Jill when they first met that she had "been married for fifteen minutes and thank God that was done." Single most of her life, Liz had a very interesting life. As mentioned before, she accumulated friendships and aided girls that needed help throughout her life. There were four girls in particular she met over her lifetime that were in various sundry circumstances. They just needed emotional and some financial support. She was financially able to help them. Liz told Jill about one of her dear friends who was very, very ill. Jill said, "She sounds ancient. She must be 80 years old."

"No, she's 56 or 57," Liz said.

"Wow, that's close to my age," Jill exclaimed.

"They are ALL your age," she said. "That was the entire point."

So, in her own way, she reached out to her daughter through women who would be about that same age. Liz left Iowa and spent most of her adult life living in Washington, D.C., and California. Nobody in Iowa except the immediate family and a few close friends knew about Liz having given birth. It wasn't talked about. In D.C. and California, she wasn't shy telling friends that she had a daughter and shared she had died at sixteen. She also told her family and Bill that her daughter had died. Bill said he didn't believe her nor did anybody else since Liz really had no way of knowing anything about her baby.

After Jill and Liz were reunited and the two became comfortable sharing more details, they were talking about Liz saying Jill had died when she was sixteen. She told Jill, "I was walking down the street, thinking about you on your birthday. I felt a horrible pain – just like someone had punched me in the stomach. I just knew you had died in a car accident."

Jill exclaimed, "You killed me off on my sixteenth birthday? Who does that?"

They both just laughed.

Jill's work required her to travel to Arizona every month so she was able to go on up to California to see Liz quite often that first year. Their reunion was in late May, so it had not been quite a year when Jill's next birthday rolled around. Her birthday happened to be on a weekend. She wanted to spend her very "first" birthday with her birth mother. But, as time approached, Liz didn't say anything. Jill spent a lot of time on adoption.com reading everything about reunions. She chatted with birth mothers and others about the best ways to develop a relationship and how the birth mothers felt. Whatever people would say about birth mothers, Jill soaked up and would ask questions of others on the website. Jill asked, "What do you think this means that she hasn't mentioned my birthday?"

Jill never got a clear answer, but she didn't want to push Liz. Jill didn't want her to do something she wasn't okay with or force the issue just because she wanted to come spend her birthday with her mother. Jill wanted her to be comfortable in the situation.

The day came when Jill had to make a plane reservation if she was going to go visit. She called and suggested she come visit Liz. Jill said, "You know, I could come out and spend my birthday with you, if you think that's a good idea. Now, if you don't, that's fine, but if you do, I would like to."

Liz nervously answered, "Oh, oh, well I hadn't really thought about that. Maybe I could do that. That sounds good. Well listen, I've got to go. Talk to you later. Bye."

Jill thought she blew it. What she didn't know was that her entire family and friends were a part of a big secret plan. Liz and Bill were throwing her a surprise birthday party for her "first" birthday. It never ever occurred to Jill that they would throw her a party. For one thing, the weekend before Jill's birthday, Bill was receiving a lifetime achievement award from an organization he had helped start. She knew he was busy. And second, Liz always told Jill that she would never travel. Liz said, "I am not coming to see you. I won't travel. Don't ask."

Little did Jill know, Liz had called Jill's best friend Jan, who Jill had known since they were ten years old. Liz had asked for her phone number to thank her for a gift and had called Jan. "I want to throw a birthday party for Jill," Liz said. "Would you be willing to put it together, invite all of her friends, and I'll pay for it?"

Jan was happy to help, and they planned this big surprise party the week before Jill's birthday, which was why Liz was so flustered when Jill called and asked to come visit her. She already was going to see Jill the week before her birthday.

Liz called Jan and in panic said, "I have to tell Jill. I know she is hurt. I must tell her. She called and wants to come here for her birthday. We are going to be there the week before. I HAVE to tell her!"

Jan said, "Bull! You are not telling her! It will be a surprise because I have worked too hard on this." She added, "Why can't Jill come out to California on her birthday, and you can have another birthday party there? Don't worry about it. Call her back. Tell her that's great."

Liz called Jill back saying okay. Jill thought it was kind of weird, but it was what she wanted and figured Liz had just got a little bit worried about everything. Maybe Liz had first felt it might be too much and then thought about it, deciding it was okay. Happily, Jill made her reservations to go.

Two or three weeks prior to the party, one of Jill's friends called and said there was an awards dinner and her husband was receiving an award. She wanted Jill to come with them. She told them that was great, and she was excited to go with them.

For the next two weeks, this friend kept reminding Jill about the dinner and asking to make sure she hadn't made any other plans. Jill told her, "Of course not. It's on my calendar. I'm not changing my plans. Why are you making this into a big deal?" But she never really thought any more about it.

The night of Jill's surprise birthday party her friends came and picked her up. "Now, keep in mind, my entire family knew about this," Jill said. "We just had celebrated Easter the week before and no one said a word."

Jill's friends took her to the place where she thought the awards dinner was being held. As she walked in and the doors open, she saw friends of hers from the small town where she raised her kids. Jill said telling the story, "There was absolutely no reason in this world that they would be at this awards ceremony, except to see me. I was just flabbergasted. I was in shock as they kind of pulled me into the room. My best friend, Jan, is there getting the biggest kick out of everything. I knew she had something to do with all of this."

Jan is an accountant just like Jill. During the spring, there is never time to celebrate. Jan said, "Well, who else do you think I would do this for? That I would plan a party during tax season!"

Jill said she laughed and thought, "Well I don't know anyone you would, I know you wouldn't throw a party if I asked you."

"As Jan said this, I saw that my future son-in-law and her son were standing side-by-side in the front of the room," Jill said. "They are big strapping guys who had played football. They stepped apart, and there were Liz and Bill smiling at me. I just lost it."

There were about fifty people there, and everyone was just getting the biggest kick out of the whole thing, clapping and cheering. Jill said she still tears up when she thinks of it. Most of her relatives, people from work, friends from all the places she had lived, and even people she had gone to grade school with were there. "You know how they say at the end your life that your life will pass before your eyes," Jill said, "Well, mine already did that night."

They had an ice sculpture that was a full circle. They had a birthday cake with a "1" first birthday candle. Jan had told everyone to bring a toy gift that reminded them of Jill so they could each tell a story about what she was like, some event it reminded them of in her life or one of her characteristics because Liz and Bill didn't know her as a little kid or her life. "Of course, there were a lot of princesses, a little toy calculator, and all kinds of things," Jill said. "Making it even more special was that all the toys were donated to a children's services in town the next day."

There were two special gifts that Jill kept. Her sister found a vintage "Chatty Cathy" doll on eBay like the one they had both enjoyed playing with for years. Jill's brother bought a vintage "Scooter" doll, the "Barbie" doll Jill had preferred. These personal gifts assured Jill that her brother and sister were excited for her and that their relationships would never change.

People got up and told story after story. Jill was totally not believing this was happening and almost in shock. Then her son, who was in college, gave a toast, "I want to toast my mom for her courage," he said. "The only reason we are here today is because she had the courage to look for something else, to find out what was there."

"It never even occurred to me that what I was doing was courageous," Jill said.

Then Bill got up and thanked everyone for being there. Bill and Liz loved hearing the stories and were so excited about everything that was going on. Then he said he wanted to toast the two people that gave them the greatest gift. He said, "I have heard stories about Alan and Ann. Jill's parents who have passed away. When Liz and I had to give up our daughter, our greatest hope was that someone would raise her and love her just like we would have. And they went beyond my wildest dreams."

What a special night that was for all of them. Like the ice sculpture, they had gone full circle even if it took fifty-one years.

Jill was with Liz on their "first" Mother's Day at church, and all the mothers and grandmothers were asked to stand. It was Liz's very first time to do so, and she stood proudly. That was a great day, and the emotion Liz felt was just amazing. This was just before the first anniversary of the day they met. An incredible, unexpected year of events had come to a close – first time they talked, first time they met, first Christmas, first meeting with Jill's children, meeting Liz's grandchildren whom Jill introduced on Liz's 70th birthday and her son's 21st birthday, Jill's first birthday, and first Mother's Day. Just after the first year was over, Liz said to Jill, "I just can't do this anymore. We can't talk. It's just too hard."

Jill was shocked. "What exactly is too hard?" she asked.

Liz said, "It brings up all the feelings of being that scared, eighteen-year-old girl with no self-esteem because I had just committed the unforgivable sin. I had humiliated my parents, cost them a lot of money, lied to my closest friends, and there was no way I could ever make this right. I just go back into being that girl that I have worked decades at forgetting."

"Thank God you are normal," Jill said.

"What?" Liz replied, "I've been carrying this around because I didn't want to hurt you."

"Well, I have been reading everything I can possibly read, and everything says it is very difficult for the birth mothers," Jill said. "It brings up all sorts of feelings."

"I know this is the best thing that has ever happened, and I should be happy all the time. This should be the greatest thing," Liz said, "but it does bring up all these old feelings."

"I know it does. That's what they say."

"You mean I am normal?"

"Yes, everybody does it."

Liz asked, "It's okay if I can be honest and tell you when it is hurting?"

"Sure, you can," Jill told her. "You don't have to say 'I don't ever want to speak to you again.' We can still talk. You can say this is difficult today, and I'll let you be. But we don't have to stop speaking to each other."

Liz was so relieved. She had no idea these were normal feelings. Even the greatest thing to happen doesn't always feel that way, and sometimes it really hurts.

It is interesting to notice how over time things change. Societal norms and acceptance is way different today than in the past. Jill and Liz experienced this firsthand about three years after their meeting. "It just so happened that my daughter was engaged and got pregnant almost in the same month that Liz had gotten pregnant with me," Jill said. "My daughter and her fiancé were trying to figure out what to do exactly. I just said, 'It just seems silly to me to wait. If you want to get married, get married. If you don't, then don't. But don't wait until the kid can walk you down the aisle to marry. Just do it.'"

Jill's daughter went ahead and got married in the fall, which would have been the same time Bill and Liz would have gotten married. Bill and Liz were both at the small wedding. Jill's adoptive parents had both passed away, and she wasn't married any longer. Since both of her kids were in the wedding, it was decided that Liz and Bill would sit with Jill. They sat on the front row at their granddaughter's wedding.

Everybody at the wedding knew Jill's daughter was pregnant and was so excited and happy for them. Liz said it was so surreal because when it happened to her, it was the biggest sin you could ever commit. You could never ever talk about it. It was the unforgivable sin. She found it interesting to see the situation and times so different. Everything was celebrated and such a joyous occasion. After the wedding, Jill's son came back down the aisle to get her and walk her out. Liz and Bill walked behind them. Liz turned and said smiling to Bill, "Better late than never."

Bill is married, and his wife is about ten years older than Jill. He has three daughters, Jill's half-sisters. They are the same age as Jill's children. Two of Bill's daughters came to the wedding. "My children have developed a close relationship with my half-sisters because they are the same age and have so much in common," Jill said. "When I walked out of the hotel elevator, it was very surreal to see Liz talking to one of my half-sisters, sharing all the stories."

Bill had been surprised when Liz first told him Jill wanted to know their medical history. He told Jill later that he didn't realize it was such a big deal until Jill's daughter sent both Liz and Bill a thank you note after her daughter was born, saying how much she appreciated them sharing their entire medical history. It was a true gift to give her daughter to have her complete medical history.

No two reunions between adoptive children and their biological parents are ever the same. Jill wants others to know when reconnecting, it isn't just the adoptive child's and birth parents' lives that are touched in a reunion. It can be extremely difficult for others. Jill's sister had it much more difficult when she found her birth mother because her parents were still alive and her birth mother had a child. She felt torn. She and Jill hid her discovery from their parents. For Jill and Liz, it was much easier because there really was no one else involved. Both of Jill's parents had passed away by then, Liz had no other children, and Jill's kids were grown. Jill's siblings were the only people who it could really affect emotionally, and they were very supportive. Bill had a more difficult time when he was told his daughter was found. His wife had always known Melanie existed, but his kids did not know about his secret. They were more affected emotionally as they began to build new relationships with these new relatives. Jill has always been grateful that Bill and his family were willing to make the effort, which wasn't always easy.

Almost four years after Jill met her birth mother, Liz was at a party. Her great granddaughter had been born, and Liz told people at the party that her life was perfect. She had her daughter, two grandchildren and now a great granddaughter. Her life was perfect. After the party as she was crossing the street in front of her home, a car hit her, and tragically she was killed. Britt and Jill were among those with her as they turned off the machines that had been keeping her alive.

It was a very intense four years Jill and Liz had together, but it was such an incredible blessing. Jill said, "Funny thing about all this, the stories I had in my head growing up about my birth parents turned out to be true. High school sweethearts. Parents told them they were too young to have a family. My birth name being Melanie and knowing I was named after Melanie from *Gone with the Wind*. All true! Most importantly, I believed that my birth mother needed to know the rest of the story. And Liz absolutely needed to know. Our reunion changed her life and gave her peace. It also changed my life and my children's and Bill's lives forever. We added additional family, and no one can have too many people who love them. As Bill told me once in the first year while we were all trying to figure out what this reunion would be, 'I cannot imagine a time when you are not a part of my life.' We all feel that way – now more than ever."

Chapter 20

Dyan's Story
(1966)

Dyan contacted me after reading My Little Valentine. *She wrote and told me that Chapter 2 could have been written about her. We became very good friends, and I knew her story needed to be shared. I visited her at her home in Texas where she shared about her experience at The Willows. She also showed me letters from friends she made there. Dyan would have been in one of the last groups of girls to live at The Willows as she was there in 1965–66, and it closed in 1969. She gives a great perspective on how it was in the latter days. It is interesting how many things at The Willows changed from when Leona was living there in 1925, while other things remained the same. Though Leona and Dyan were forty years apart, their stories are so similar.*

Dyan's story began January 31,1949, in Burlington, Iowa, where she was born. When Dyan was two, her family moved to Quincy, Illinois. She was a "tom boy," dragging all kinds of animals home, including snakes, much to the consternation of her mother. She laughed telling me she was precocious, saying her mother probably would have used a much different word to describe her. Dyan and her mother were polar opposites. Her mother was a prim and proper school teacher, and she was a young girl full of ideas of life and adventure. Dyan was also a daddy's girl. She loved her dad and would have done anything to try and please him. Her older brother was the apple of her mother's eye. He could do no wrong. Dyan said, "He went off to college and didn't even know what was happening with the rest of our family during my turbulent time."

The relationship Dyan had with her mother hit a low point in 1965 when she was just sixteen years old. Her bubbly and outgoing personality made her a popular social butterfly. Though she had good grades at school, her interactions with her girlfriends were by far more important than school. She had a relationship with an older boy who was her brother's good friend. In the sixties, it still was such taboo to have sex outside of marriage and definitely no one talked about it. When she realized she was pregnant, she was scared to death. She had no idea what to do or who to tell. Eventually she had to tell her parents. Her mother was mortified. What would the family and neighbors think? She made the decision right then and there not to tell her family who the father was. That would only cause more problems. Dyan said, "The boy never acknowledged my being pregnant. Years later at a group meeting, he told me it wasn't until I had to go away that it dawned on him that he was the father."

Dyan's father was supportive and on her side. Her dad wanted her to be able to keep the baby, and the family would raise it. But her mom would have nothing to do with that. Her pregnancy caused a lot of fighting in their home. Dyan said she just wanted to run away. She really didn't know what her parents did or who they talked to, but shortly after the news was divulged, she found herself on a train heading to Kansas City.

Her parents told her she was going to a home for unwed mothers. Some place called The Willows Maternity Sanitarium. The date was October 26, 1965, when she arrived with her father at the doorstep of the huge stately Victorian mansion near the railway station. There was a grand foyer entrance with an office for the admissions on one side. The other side was the office of Mrs. Haworth, or Garnet, as Dyan said the girls called her.

Dyan remembers how scared she was; she was literally shaking. She said she felt lost as if her whole world was flipped upside down. She was shown to what would be her room for the next several months. She met her roommate "Carol," who was in college studying botany. This of course was not her real name. Most of the girls went by fake names for privacy, although Dyan used her real name, not caring if others knew. Carol shared that she and her boyfriend had decided they couldn't raise a baby while in college. They would put it up for adoption. They were still a couple and planned to get married once they got their degrees. Dyan said, "We truly had nothing in common, well I take that back, we both were victims of unfortunate circumstances that brought us to this shared room."

Their room was pleasant enough with simple furniture and decor but nothing to write home about. There were two iron-framed beds, two desks with chairs, and a dresser they shared. Later that day, Dyan was taken to the basement where she was instructed that she could pick out some of the maternity clothes to wear that were hanging from lines or folded in clothes baskets. As she grew in girth, she would swap out for larger sizes. When girls were ready to go home, they would drop these very unflattering garbs in the chutes that went to the basement to the laundry to be washed and recycled to the next girls. Dyan said laughing, "I wonder if any of the same clothes Leona wore were still there. Some were pretty out of date."

She said there was one particular blouse she chose that she thought was so cute. She packed it with her own clothes and took it back home. When she returned to Illinois, her mother was not happy that she brought home this maternity blouse and the remembrance it gave of the situation never to be mentioned again. Her mother destroyed the blouse.

Dyan's time at The Willows provided some memories that have stayed with her all these many years later, while others are just a blur. She said all the girls felt shame and unbearable loneliness back in those days. She never forgot the humiliation she felt as a naive sixteen-year-old girl when she was given her weekly pelvic exam by the house doctor. Usually there would be several young male interns from the nearby hospital along with the doctor to participate in the exam. She said with her legs uncovered and exposed, she was devastated. She would just have to go into a Zen-like or numb state of mind to survive the embarrassment. She felt as if she was being punished for her sins.

Outside of The Willows was an oval walkway made of concrete called "the bullpen." There was a towering oak tree in the middle with a picnic table and plenty of friendly squirrels just waiting for a handout. Girls walked round and round the oval, or they sat and chatted. She was at The Willows in the winter about the same time of year as Leona so only on the warmer days did she get to spend time at the bullpen.

Dyan had never lived away from home before she went to The Willows. Two major holidays, Thanksgiving and Christmas, occurred during her time there. "Dad and Mom decided to visit at Thanksgiving and brought my brother," Dyan said. "I was worried about looking pregnant in front of my family so I put a girdle on and wore a dark sweater to hide my baby bump, which was actually more like a mountain. When my brother came in, he said 'Where is it?' referring to my baby." Dyan added, "Mrs. Haworth very graciously set us up in a room off the front door with a pull curtain for privacy. She had Thanksgiving dinner brought to us as we sat at a card table. It was a very somber day. Who knows what we talked about. I don't even remember the taste of the food. It was like having an out-of-body moment."

Carol said her brother remembers he was saddened and shocked because he didn't know anything until he came home from school. "He probably had an out-of-body experience, too."

MANSION ON A HILL

Dyan shared that the food at The Willows was pretty good. "Except when they served tongue! The poached eggs were great," she said. "I had my own salt shaker to season the food." She remembers, "The gal who was the cook or kitchen help was a black lady and had the warmest smile."

Being a teacher, Dyan's mother provided her with books and studies during her stay at The Willows so she didn't fall behind. Mrs. Haworth made sure Dyan did her school work. She was able to graduate with her class in 1967. She proudly sent Mrs. Haworth a graduation announcement. Dyan kept the letter she received back from Mrs. Haworth.

June 12, 1967

Dear Miss Merkel:

It was so nice of you to remember me with one of your graduation announcements. It is a great occasion and I know you must be very happy, and your parents very proud of you.

I hope you will have a full measure of happiness through the years to come and with my kindest personal regards to all of you, I am.

Sincerely,

Garnet M. Haworth

Dyan's High School Photo from 1966-67
Photo courtesy of Dyan Merkel

The Willows' girls were very social and became fast friends. All the girls went by their first names, real or fake but never used last names. They were "Haworth" girls and the unity and common bond they felt were very strong. They only had each other. Dyan said, "Garnet took us sad and scared young girls into her 'home' and showered us with affection though she was stern and set very strict rules. She encouraged us to overlook this little bump in the road and to make something of our lives upon returning home."

Once a week the girls were allowed to leave and go shopping at the Plaza, to a movie, or do some other activity. This was a definite change from earlier years when girls were not allowed to socialize or leave the facility. Dyan loved to go to the Hallmark Mall and buy yarn. She was a prolific knitter. "I bought so much yarn and knitted lots of sweaters," Dyan said. "I loved the sweaters and gave so many to my friends and family. I could whip one out in a day. I was my own little factory. My dad was sweet to send me money to shop."

Being the social butterfly, Dyan developed several close friendships. After giving birth and returning home, she received many letters from friends still at The Willows. One of her dearest friends named Linda wrote this letter to her about a trip out on the town that got her and a new girl in hot water with Mrs. Haworth.

> *Dyan,*
>
> *A week ago, Thursday, Sherry, the new girl, and I went to the Plaza. We shopped all day and at 3:30 went to the Plaza III for a drink. Before we knew it, the time was 4:45 p.m. and so we tried to call Mrs. Haworth. We couldn't get her so we decided to stay out for dinner. I had a delicious lobster dinner and was still a little high (excited) when we returned here at 7:30 p.m. Mrs. Haworth was waiting for us and madder than a wasp. She won't let me go out for four weeks and Sherry couldn't go out for a week. Not only did we stay out past 4:00, but we also forgot to sign out and get nurse's permission. Really absent-minded, aren't I? It was worth it though because we had a ball. This is the first time I've been punished for getting in at 7:30 p.m. It could only happen at The Willows.*

There was one desperately sad and withdrawn girl at The Willows whom Dyan assumed was in her late teens. She never ever spoke to anyone and just stayed in her room except for meals. The rumor mill, which ironically ran rampant at The Willows, was that this was the little waif's third visit to The Willows. Adding horror to the whispered story was the scandal that the girl's own father was the babies' father. Dyan never knew if the gossip was really true.

Dyan reached her seventeenth birthday at The Willows in January 1966 with little fanfare or hoopla (much the same as Leona celebrating her birthday on December 27, 1924). Although one big difference, Dyan's parents were able to call and wish her a happy birthday. She said, "At the time I felt huge and bloated – just like the Goodyear blimp. What a somber place to spend one's seventeenth birthday."

Dyan was miserable. Time went at a very slow pace. She just wanted this over with, but she also knew as long as she carried her baby inside her, she wouldn't have to give it up. Once a girl went into labor, she was taken to the confinement room never to be seen again by the girls who had not delivered yet. Later Dyan understood it was to prevent horror stories of childbirth from being spread to the still pregnant, naive girls.

One week after her birthday, Dyan's baby decided it was time to enter the world. After her water broke, she was taken to the confinement room where she spent an eternity in labor. Mrs. Haworth and several of the nurses took turns sitting with her. The doctor was contacted after she was fully dilated. The contractions came quicker and with more intensity. The pain was intensified exponentially. She said it was like her hips were being torn apart, but she was told not to scream and scare the other girls. Needles scared her to death, but they gave her a spinal before they did an episiotomy. Nothing in her birthing classes at The Willows came close to preparing her for the pain that she felt during and after labor.

This cute cartoon drawing of a smiling baby in the womb came from a popular series of books about Eggbert and Eggberta in the 1960s. It was used in the girls' anatomy health class. It did little to prepare or express the pain in the actual event. Dyan said, "I know I shouldn't have kept the little drawing from the class, but I hid it in my books. Of course, my mom never saw it. I have kept it all these years."

Eggbert Cartoon
Drawing courtesy of Dyan Merkel

Dyan's baby girl was born on February 7, 1966. She was taken from her immediately, and she was not allowed to hold or nurse her at that time. She did get to see her baby three times. A friend of Dyan's named Linda, who was a little older and also one of Garnet's girls, worked in the nursery during her stay at The Willows. She snuck Dyan into the nursery to see her baby against Mrs. Haworth's rules. There was a little room with only a rocking chair at the top of some itsy-bitsy stairs. Dyan remembers almost tripping going up. She was able to rock her baby and give her a bottle. Dyan said, "My baby girl was such a beautiful baby with lots of blonde hair pulled up in a little ponytail on top of her head. My heart forever would love my little girl."

The next day, Dyan was given a shot that was to help stop lactation. She had no idea what it was they gave her. (It was probably a bromocriptine shot, which was often given automatically in hospitals during the 1960s and 70s to dry up a mother's milk. In 1994 the FDA banned bromocriptine due to risk of cancer and stroke.) Her now much larger breasts were wrapped tight and pads inserted into her clothing under her armpits. This seventeen-year-old young woman could not avoid acknowledging her body fighting the motherly instincts the nurses wanted to take away.

"I felt as if my still bloated body was a sieve, and the liquid was pouring out of every pore under my armpits," Dyan said. "I was nauseous and felt mixed emotions of guilt, depression, sadness, relief, and anguish all sweeping over my body in a compiled mishmash of confusion. No understanding of postpartum depression in those days." She continued, "The idea of wanting to keep my baby flooded my thoughts, but I had long signed over my rights to keep my little baby girl when I had entered the hallowed doors of The Willows."

After her daughter was born, Mrs. Haworth asked Dyan what she was going to name her baby girl. "I thought my daughter should have a special name," Dyan said. "I always loved the actress Greta Garbo, and I wanted my daughter to be as beautiful. So, I named her Greta."

Just a couple days after she had given birth, Dyan was confronted with the dreaded signing of the birth certificate in court, sharing the name she had chosen, and asked to give the father's name. Mrs. Joan Nichols, The Willow's court appointed social worker, rode with Dyan by taxi to court. Dyan remembered how horrible that ride was. She was still so sore from giving birth and the episiotomy. She felt every bounce. "Mrs. Nichols was a sweet and compassionate lady," Dyan said. "She always dressed extremely well, especially I thought for a social worker. It was February and cold the day we went to court. Mrs. Nichols had on a beautiful short mink coat. When we got to the courthouse to my surprise, Mrs. Nichols took her mink coat off and put it on the chair for me to sit on because she knew how uncomfortable I was. I will never forget her kindness toward me."

Mrs. Nichols emphasized to Dyan that she had up to six months to change her mind and claim her baby, even after a couple chose to adopt baby Greta. It did give her hope that she might get to keep her baby, but she knew in her heart this wasn't ever going to be an option for her. When the question came about the father of the baby for the birth certificate, Dyan hedged. "I refused to give the real father's name and lied as to who the father was. I used a made-up name of someone no one would find. Trust me, my mother tried everything."

Within what seemed just a few hours after court, she found herself on a train with her father heading home to Illinois and had this little "bump in the road" smoothed out to be forgotten, at least that is what she was told. The train ride could be described in one word—miserable. Her body's reaction to giving birth, the episiotomy, and the shot tormented her for the several hours trip. She was dripping wet under her armpits from the water weight being expelled from her body.

Once home, Dyan's mother was still unhappy with her. She told Dyan in no uncertain terms not to tell anyone about her situation. Her mom had been telling everyone that she was sick and had to go get treatment. She told others that her daughter's increased size was reaction to the medicine she had to take. Within just a few days of returning home, her mother sent her back to school. Once at school, Dyan told her very close group of girlfriends the whole truth about giving birth to Greta. She didn't care what her mother had told her to say. Her friends loved her and supported her. To this day, these high school girlfriends and Dyan are still very close. They get together every few years for a reunion and go away to some beautiful beach on the Atlantic coast.

It was a horrible time in her home life when she returned home. Before going to The Willows was no picnic, but now Dyan felt she was seen even more as the bad seed. Her parents separated and divorced. Her mother blamed her for the divorce. And her brother was drafted into the service. Dyan and her mother were stuck in the same bad relationship without a referee. Upon returning home, she kept in touch with her girlfriends at The Willows and shared her struggles. It was comforting to know there were others who understood what she was going through. Her friend, Linda, wrote her several times. In one of Linda's letters she comforted Dyan by writing and giving sage advice.

Dyan,

I was sorry to hear that you and your mother weren't getting along. I know you expected as I will too, that when you returned home your parents would try to make you as happy as possible. It would be nice if they welcomed us with open arms, but we aren't being too realistic, are we? They've been hurt and have really suffered more than we. It's no wonder why they may feel a little resentment and hurt for a long while. Just try to be patient, understanding, and learn to bite your tongue instead of fighting back. Oh, I know it's easy enough for me to say, but honestly, I know how you feel and it will be easier on you if you try to take the cutting remarks and limitations they may place on you.

When I was in high school, my mother was going through her change of life and was very irritable. She was nervous and we fought constantly. When I look back, she was right many, many times and if only I had kept my mouth shut, we would have gotten along so much better. Try to be patient Dyan, and gripe to me instead of to your folks or instead of keeping it inside. Just think, it won't be long before you'll be off to college and on your own.

While she was at The Willows, Dyan's grandmother became very ill and passed away on February 11 before she got home. She was heartbroken that she never got to see her or say goodbye. Her funeral was shortly after Dyan returned home. Linda wrote saying:

I can't imagine having to go to a funeral on my eighth day. UGH! We bet you were really sore.

MANSION ON A HILL

Linda and her boyfriend Kurt remained a couple as far as Dyan knew. They were hiding her pregnancy from both of their parents. They still wanted to get married but didn't feel they were ready to have a child. Linda pretended to be teaching in Kansas City. She was at The Willows longer than anyone else Dyan knew, arriving shortly after her first month of pregnancy. "It really is amazing how close we all became and the connection that was made," Dyan said. "With so many different backgrounds and such difference in ages, we bonded because of our common circumstance we were sharing. We encouraged one another, and I really don't know how we would have made it through our ordeals without each other. We truly developed a sisterhood."

As can be seen by this next letter from Linda, the girls continued to stay in touch and were truly interested in knowing how each other was doing. Because Linda worked in the nursery part time, she had access to Greta and kept Dyan informed. She also shared how the other girls were doing and recovering from childbirth.

February 23, 1966

Dear Dyan,

I was so happy to get your letter. I have lots of news to tell you.

First of all, Susie delivered a boy after two hours of labor. She looked great when she left and called the other night to say she'd been out with a fellow for a ride. She felt so funny and wouldn't let him kiss her good night.

Tina was the next to go on February 15. She started getting pains at 7:00 p.m. and had a little girl at 10:15 p.m. She named her Tonya. She said she'd write to you after she leaves on Friday with her parents. They're going to Arizona for a week. She looks great and is sitting fairly well. Donna started having pains Saturday afternoon. She went to the labor room at 7:00 p.m. and also delivered at 10:15 p.m. that night. She had a girl and named her Sharon. One hour after she got into convalescence, she was walking around and had dinner at the table on second. Today she almost looked normal and has recovered so quickly. I was really surprised Susie called her baby, Jerry. Connie is still waiting and is now a week overdue.

I'm now working in the nursery every other day. Little Greta is so pretty and don't worry, I'm taking good care of her.

A new girl came the Sunday after you left. She's 23 and was an airline stewardess. She's really nice and is due after me. Now I don't feel so badly.

Just two days after you left a new girl arrived from Quincy. She's about 18 and no one has mentioned your name to her. I don't think anyone else realizes that you two are from the same town. It was lucky that she came after you left.

Linda didn't get the letter finished and added the rest of this long letter a few days later.

February 26, 1966

Connie delivered a girl last night about 8:00 and Martha delivered this a.m. She had a girl and was three weeks early. She was such a nice girl and I'm glad she got to go early. Tina left yesterday and Donna leaves tonight. The place is really going to be quiet without the old group around. Tina had tears in her eyes when she left.

Our new cook arrived and she's really good. We've had delicious desserts every night. Last night chocolate cake and chocolate meringue pie today. Big pieces too! Only thing is, I've already gained five pounds and Mrs. Kramer is having a fit.

Don't feel badly about your measurements – mine will probably be the same or worse! I'm trying to lose weight as I want to visit Kurt at the end of March if I'm not showing. It's his birthday and maybe (??) I'll get my diamond ring too!! I'll let you know, if I do. Besides I miss him so much and can't stand this place without a break.

Well, Dyan, I haven't anymore news. I hope you're caught up on your studies and being a good girl. Write again soon and you should be getting a letter from Tina soon.

Love,

Linda

P.S. You thought Tina was kidding when she said I wrote long letters, but as you can see by the (8) on top of this page, I am a little wordy.

P.S.S I'll be looking for your next letter.

A couple weeks later, Linda wrote again sharing about the happenings at The Willows. More importantly, she gave Dyan additional information about Greta. That meant the world to Dyan.

March 16, 1966

Dear Dyan,

Sorry that I'm late in answering your letter, but believe it or not, I've been busy. Working in the nursery is really helping to make the time fly and I'm also trying to finish the sweater for Kurt. I only have one more sleeve to do.

Tina is back at home now and as yet doesn't have a job. She and her mother aren't getting along too well either. She is thinking seriously of going into the airlines. Donna has called several times and is so depressed and lonely. She has moved out of her house and into an apartment because she and her folks couldn't get along at all. She interviewed with several airlines and was offered one job with Mohawk Airlines flying out of New York. She interviews with American Airlines this Friday. I know once she starts working she will be happier but right now all she can think about is her baby. Her grandmother wants her to come back and get her baby which wouldn't be a good thing at all. I don't think she will because deep down she realized this wouldn't be the best thing for Sharon or her. As I've said before, a girl ought to close this part of her life out when she leaves here and try and forget it. I hope she gets busy and forgets about her baby.

Betty delivered a boy a few days ago and had a short labor. Doris is still waiting and is overdue. She's been confined to bed for about two weeks because of high blood pressure. She's really eating that up to be sure. It's kind of funny because she always thought she was such an expert on when people would deliver.

I can't remember if I gave you the telephone number here in my last letter but it is PL-39723. I'd love to talk to you sometime.

How's school coming? Did you make cheerleading? I sure hope so because you'd be so good and you sure should have made it. I don't know how you ever did the splits just after you'd gotten home.

MANSION ON A HILL

No one has heard from Susie, but Donna said she was in Indiana. Oh, Donna's brother told all his friends about why she was there. Isn't that nice! What a family she has.

We've got several new girls here that are also due in July. It sure seems nice not to be the last one due. There are some really sharp and nice girls here now so it's not so bad.

I'm still hoping to go back to Michigan at the end of this month, but only for a few days. I'm showing a little but I hope with a good girdle I'll look normal. I want to see Kurt so badly, but I'm a little scared someone will get smart and say I look different. Problems, problems!

I haven't gone out for four weeks and I'm beginning to go a little buggy. I'm still not getting along with Mrs. Haworth too well. She's so phony and I try to stay clear of her.

Well I can't think of anymore news. I hope you and your folks are getting along better. Keep your chin up and keep smiling and everything will work out alright. Greta is so pretty and is beginning to look more like you. She doesn't smile a lot, but when she does, it's so cute.

I hope you're well and please write soon. Let me know how you and that fellow are getting along. Sounds like he's a nice guy and I hope he's sincere. Don't be fooled though and keep your distance until you know you're in love with him and vice versa. Maggie says "hi" and I'll say goodbye for now.

Love,

Linda

Dyan didn't hear from Linda for a few months, and then she got this letter updating what was going on at The Willows and her life with Kurt. She always encouraged Dyan and was like a big sister to her.

May 6, 1966

Dear Dyan,

I'm sorry that I haven't written in so long. I have been busy though believe it or not. Last week I typed a term paper for Mrs. O'Neal. It was 21 pages long and had 29 footnotes, so that kept me busy every afternoon. Kurt's sweater has been so hard to put together. I'd get stuck on something and have to wait a week before I could get downtown to ask the Macy's instructor how to go on. It is all done now and tomorrow I'm sending it out to be blocked. I'm so proud of it and am starting one for my Dad now. I guess Kurt will have to wait until next winter to wear it though.

Maggie and I have been roommates since Tina left and we have a TV. Therefore, every night we watch it and I'm getting so sick of the old movies and stupid shows. Things are about the same here except we can now go out two times a week. The "bullpen" is beginning to look very pretty and I've been sitting out there every morning and part of the afternoons. Yesterday I got quite a burn and hope to be nice and tan by the time I go home.

Nora has gone home. She left yesterday and really looked nice. She weighs about 175 lbs., which was quite a weight loss for her. She changed a lot here and became quite a lovely girl. She had a little girl. Betty also left several weeks ago. She had a boy. Susie called last week and said she was fine. She hadn't stopped her period though and might have to have a D and C. Donna hasn't written in a long time, but the last I talked with her, she was miserable. A lot of her problems, she created herself, I think. Mrs. Haworth has been very nice to us lately. This weekend she went to the Kentucky Derby.

We can't order out anymore though as she found out about it. She couldn't really penalize us though as there were too many of us who were guilty. Doris also had a girl and has left. She and her boyfriend aren't getting along, I hear. I'm not too surprised.

I'm so proud of you for being elected treasurer of your class. What an honor! Have you decided where you'll go to college yet? You must go, Dyan, because they will be the best years of your life. I promise you that! I'm also glad to know you've found happiness with your boyfriend. Just keep playing things coolly though as you have a long time before you should get tied down and serious. My ideas and taste in boys changed so much after I went to college. So, wait before you really commit yourself and see how you feel when you get to college and meet other fellas.

Mrs. Ghain has left. She quit shortly after you left. She comes back to visit every so often though and may work again when Mrs. Kramer goes to England this summer. She didn't like her hours and wasn't feeling well either.

Kurt and I are fine. We are still planning on a Sept. or Oct. wedding. I went home at the end of March to see him for a week. I had such a good time and it was good I went then because shortly after I got back I started showing. Now I look like I really belong here and I hate this new shape. I can hardly wait to go home and the time is beginning to drag. "Uncle Sam" is *breathing down Kurt's neck and we can't make any real definite plans until we hear definitely about when he'll have to go into the service. My folks are crazy about him and now know that we are planning to get married. My mother bought me my silver already as part of my wedding present. My pattern is "Contessina by Towle." Also, Mom still doesn't know why I'm here. She believes I'm teaching and thank God, she hasn't asked any questions. I only hope she'll never have to know.*

Well I can't think of anymore news. I'm so glad you're going to visit in May. I can hardly wait to see your new figure. Sounds great! (Dyan did not end up going back to visit.) *I hope you're studying hard for your finals and being good. Stay happy and write again soon. I'll see you soon, I hope.*

Love,

Linda

    There was one common thread the girls all shared, they craved acceptance and all worried about their futures and figures. Dyan said they worried they would never have another boyfriend or find someone. Her friend Tina wrote not too long after she returned home. She struggled with giving up her baby and was pressured by her boyfriend's family to get back with him. She had to go to court to get the matter resolved. "I can't imagine going through what she did," Dyan said.

    Tina wrote in a couple letters about the ordeal and how incredibly Mrs. Haworth had supported her. She shared about her old boyfriend and how much she still loved him.

March 21, 1966

Dear Dyan,

MANSION ON A HILL

I'm sorry I haven't written, but time has really gone fast.

Boy, I really had trouble after you left. Jack's mother called all week and wanted me to give her the baby. Well I told her I went with Tonya and that was that!

Tonya weighed 6 lbs 15 oz. and 19 inches long. She was real cute.

I was only in labor 3 hours and hard labor about 45 mins. Not bad.

I'm going to college in the fall and now I'm working for my father in the office.

How are you and your mother getting along? My mother and I are getting along pretty fair. We argue a lot about little things.

Oh, yes, there was all sorts of gossip going around about me and it's really funny some of the rumors.

Have you had any dates yet? I haven't but some guys are asking about me.

Have you lost much weight yet? I weigh 127 and I can't seem to lose anymore. My measurements are 38-24-38. Boy, how does that sound?

Are you still knitting? I gave it up for "Lent!" (Just kidding) I gave it up completely. It reminds me too much of Kansas City. Well I must go. It's 1:00 a.m. and I must get some sleep. Always, Tina

P.S. Write!

KELLEE PARR

Only ten days later Tina wrote:

March 31, 1966

Dear Dyan,

I'm at work now. Boy am I tired. I went to New York City yesterday morning at 5:15 and got home at 9:00 last night. I'm just beat!

My cousin and I went looking for gowns for her wedding. I'm maid of honor. It's June 24. Our gowns are just beautiful. They're all white with violet trim. Floor length. They are real sharp.

I haven't heard from Linda since I left Kansas City. I don't know why I haven't heard from her. I wrote four letters to her and sent a box and she never wrote. I'm plenty mad.

I haven't had any dates yet because all the kids are at college. But, will be home for Easter. On Tuesday night, this guy asked my cousin (the nosey one) if she thought I would go out with him. She said she thought I would. He's 26 and loaded with money, but he's not Jack. I still feel an awful lot for him. I guess I always will.

Well about Jack's mother, she called up my fourth day, Feb. 18 and said Jack had just told her I was P.G. and she wanted me and Tonya to come to KY and live with "her" and them. Maybe Jack would take me back. Well I told her to forget the whole thing. I said "if" Jack loves me, he'll call and ask me without his mother's help! She didn't like that too much. Then I talked to his brother, who is 25 and married and has 2 boys, one 6 months and one 4 years. He said he was going to talk to Jack and see if he couldn't work things out. He really wanted to help me and Tonya and Jack. He said not to give up hope yet. Well that Saturday Jack's mother's lawyer called Mrs. Haworth and wanted to talk to me. She wouldn't let me, THANK GOD!! At that point, I was a nervous wreck. This went on all week till I went to court. I was going crazy. Now it's all over and I'm glad. I hated to leave Tonya. I felt like I left part of me behind and I still feel that way. I'll never forget Feb.15 ever.

I was 21½ hours overdue. Not very long, hah!! And I didn't have hardly any trouble. Only 3 hours of labor all together. Donna only had 1 hour 35 minutes of labor. Lucky girl. Enough of that!

I got my Easter outfit. It cost me $145.00 in all. I don't care. It's great buying clothes again! It's hot pink coat and suit with a big hat with light green and pink in it and light green shoes and purse. It's really beautiful.

I'm only down to 125 pounds but I haven't done any exercises yet! My doctor is sick and I can't go for my 6 weeks check-up yet.

I hope this letter is longer because my hand is aching! I'm getting my ears pierced on Saturday. I'm a little scared.

Well I better close. Write real soon. I really do hope we can get together sometime soon in the near future.

Love,

Tina

It does seem young people can bounce back quite quickly. Dyan received this letter two months after Tina's last letter. She seemed to have recovered from her broken heart. Jack was out of the picture for good and replaced by Tom. Obviously, Tina had not been ready to be a mother. Dyan said, "I had to laugh when I got this letter from her. Tina was quite a pistol."

June 8, 1966

Dear Dyan,

Sorry I haven't written to you in such a long time, but I've been very busy getting ready for my cousins wedding. She is getting married on June 15 and I'm her maid of honor. We are wearing white gowns with purple trimming. They are beautiful!

Well let me tell you about Memorial Day weekend. My cousin Bonnie (the one I'm in her wedding), we went to Washington D.C. for Friday till Monday. Well, I went out with Bonnie's future nephew Tom. Well what a DOLL. We really hit it off and we are dating steadily now. He has blond hair, he's 24 years old, has his own motor boat and drives a '65 Chevy. He works for IBM in Trenton, New Jersey. He is really tuff and I really care quite a bit for him. Jack means nothing to me now. Tom is so much more than Jack could ever be. Well, this past weekend he came up to my house and my parents just love him and so does he (love my parents that is.) This weekend he is coming up again. I just count the days and it's only two days and 15 hours.

Did you go to Kansas City to see the girls yet? Linda said you were coming. I called her about a month ago and I talked to Maggie and Sherry. They sounded really happy. They sure put on a good act. Like we did. Oh brother!

Are you still dating the guy you were when I heard from you last? Are you going with anyone new?

About my weekend in D.C. Oh brother!!!! On Friday night, we went to a place called the Monkey Business. And got home at 4:30 in the morning. And Saturday night we went to a Cocktail Party and I got bombed out of my mind and got home about 4:00. Sunday night we went to some more nightclubs and got in at 3:00. Monday we slept till about 10:30 and got Tom up and went to a Park called Great Falls. What a weekend. I'm still not over it and never will be, because every weekend with Tom we never get in till the wee hours of the morning. Which I don't mind when I'm with him.

I start Business College in the fall. I'm really sick of working and can't wait till I start college.

Well I weigh 115 pounds now and I just bought a new bathing suit and got a size 7. Can you believe it, me in a size 7?

Well, I must go. I'm at work and my dad just walked in. Sooooooooooooooooooooooo, bye for now. Write real soon.

Love,

Tina

Toward the end of March, Dyan received more information about Greta and her placement in her new adoptive home. Though sad, it gave Dyan peace of mind knowing her baby girl was in a good home. She still had five months to change her mind, but she knew Greta was in a much better home than she could give. Mrs. Joan Nichols, the social worker, wrote the following letter.

KELLEE PARR

March 22, 1966

Dearest Diana, (misspelled Dyan's name)

The good news for you at last that Greta is with her new parents and they have shown to be wonderful, as we previously placed a boy with them. They reside outside N.C., are Protestant and the father is head of a branch of a large national concern. Their home reflects refinement and culture. They both take active part in Church and Civic affairs. The mother excels in sewing and is most creative. She will have the utmost in love and security.

Hope all is going well for you and that your plans for the future is working out just the way you had planned. Think of you often.

All is as busy as ever around here.

Love and luck always,

Joan Nichols

After graduating from high school, Dyan went on to college, though not to be a teacher or nurse as her mother would have preferred. She went into the arts and wanted to use her creative side. She went to Southern Illinois University. Even with working two jobs, she ran out of money so she quit school. Eventually Dyan got married, but she was not ready to have children after the traumatic experience she went through as a teenager. She didn't feel worthy of another child at that time. Just like Leona, she never forgot the daughter she had to leave in Kansas City. Dyan has only since been back to Kansas City one time in 1980 and drove by 2929 Main Street. "My heart sank when I saw The Willows was gone," she said.

MANSION ON A HILL

Dyan divorced and eventually remarried. This time her husband didn't want to have children when she was finally ready to have another child. They divorced and Greta was to be Dyan's only child.

All of her life Dyan loved animals, especially dogs and horses. She said growing up in the city, pets were not allowed in their house. It was no place to have an animal, according to her mom. Dyan loved hanging out at her girlfriend's farm or just any farm as long as it was country and had animals. "My love for animals led to a life of raising top German shepherd dogs," Dyan said. "These dogs have become my children. Most of my dogs I have bred and raised myself. I'm so very proud to be the breeder of the most beautiful female who was the Futurity, Maturity winner and 1982 Grand Victrix Champion Merkel's Vendetta ROM. I have also imported world class dogs from Germany and widely traveled showing dogs. It is a life I have so loved which helped me deal with my loss and helped me from being lonely. Not everyone gets me and my love for these animals, but my dogs do. That is all that matters."

In the late 1990s, Dyan was elated when she found out her daughter Greta (who was renamed Susan at adoption) was looking for her. It was what she had prayed for. They were reunited, and she found out she had three beautiful grandchildren, two boys and a girl. Dyan has been able to develop a relationship with her daughter and her grandchildren. She beamed with pride when she spoke of Susan, who is a pediatric nurse practitioner. Dyan is so proud of her daughter's accomplishments in life.

Her oldest grandson and his wife came to Dyan's house to get a puppy (their first child) and just returned for another. She shared that her grandchildren are all incredible young adults. She was so happy that her parents were able to meet and spend twelve years with their great grandchildren.

Toward the end of her mother's life, Dyan and her mother became quite close. It wasn't until years later after her mom came to live in Texas that she learned some things about her mother's life and began to put some understanding behind the up and down relationship the two of them had over their lifetimes. "It always seemed like I was making my mother the bad person, but she was a victim of her society and lacked the understanding of positive reinforcement in raising her own children," Dyan said.

Dyan didn't know until her mother shared that she and her siblings had suffered years of abuse in her family. Dyan's grandfather's drinking forced the older children to leave and find their own way. Many times the police were called. The last time broke up the family. He beat Dyan's grandmother and broke her jaw. The court ordered the remaining three children (including Dyan's mother) into an orphanage. Dyan's mother admitted going into the orphanage was the best thing that ever happened to her. However, the younger sister kept getting in trouble at the orphanage, and Dyan's mother was worried about losing this home, too. When her mother opened up about her upbringing, she shared that Dyan's similarity to her aunt brought back those tough times. Dyan said sadly, "I think it kept her from appreciating me as much as she would have liked."

Dyan continued, "My grandfather adored me. He looked forward to our visits so we could have a beer (Busch longneck bottle) and watermelon. We would walk to the corner bar to fill his jug. We would sit at the bar and the bartender would give me a little glass of draft beer and Grandpa would have a normal glass."

Their close relationship was very difficult for her mother. Dyan said, "Even with the dysfunctional relationship with her father, my mother told me how much she had wanted her father to acknowledge her like he did me. That broke my heart."

Her mother told Dyan one day that she reminded her of her mother, whom she loved dearly. It was uplifting for Dyan to have her mother give her a heartfelt compliment.

When Dyan's mother became ill and was in the ICU dying, Susan and her husband came to Texas. (Susan went years earlier to Dyan's father's funeral in Quincy.) Susan went to the hospital by herself. She sat next to her birth grandmother and read to her. Dyan said, "When we had to agree to turn off her respirator, I struggled to sign off. I was the last holdout. One thing was for sure. I didn't want her to die on Susan's birthday, February 7. My mother passed on February 10, 2012. It was one day before my grandmother died, who died in 1966 when I was at The Willows."

Today, Dyan has two wishes, two things she feels would make her live complete. For her first wish she said, "Susan is the only baby I have held in my entire life. I am looking forward to holding a great grandchild one day if I am so blessed."

Her second wish is she would like to have the opportunity to meet the adoptive mother of her baby girl. Susan and her husband invited Dyan to join them for Easter one year. Dyan was not able to go because she could find no one to take care of her dogs, but she also worried it might be uncomfortable for Susan's adoptive mother if she joined them. Susan's husband said not to worry, she wasn't like that at all. Dyan still hopes to meet her. She is in her eighties. Dyan said, "I would like to thank Susan's adoptive mother one day for giving my daughter the wonderful home life and financial opportunity to be the best she could be."

Meeting Susan and developing a relationship with her and her family has meant so much to Dyan. She said, "So, the worst time in my life became the best thing in my life. I feel blessed."

Chapter 21

Nancy's Story (1966)

Nancy and I met through the Willows' Facebook page. I appreciate all I have learned from her about life at The Willows. Her stay at The Willows was one of the longest I have heard of as she entered in early October 1965 and was there through April 1966. Her son Chad was born April 3, 1966. She always hoped to meet him one day but felt very strongly it was not her place to search for him. She did not want to interfere or interrupt his life. She felt she relinquished that right when she gave him away. She knows not everyone feels the same way but that is her strong belief. I wish to thank Nancy for her insight into what The Willows was like in its final years and how things changed.

Nancy was a student at a college for women in Colorado. After she discovered she was pregnant, she went to the Dean's office and told her the situation. She said, "Well, we can fix that, Nancy."

She told her she didn't think they could. The Dean said for her to just go on over to the infirmary, and they could take care of it. Nancy said there was no way she would do that. She got a ride back home to Nebraska and told her parents. They panicked. She and her mother flew off to Portland to stay with an aunt until arrangements could be made at The Willows. She said it was like, "Get her out of the state to not bring shame on the family even though it wasn't her fault."

MANSION ON A HILL

They flew directly from Portland to Kansas City where she would stay the next seven months. At the airport, they were met by a very proper, gray-haired, stout lady named Mrs. Haworth. She asked Nancy her name, and she was told there was already a Nancy staying at The Willows so her name from that point on was "Sandy." "Everyone there only knew me by that name," Nancy said. "To this day I hear that name being called out – I turn my head."

Nancy remembers all the way on the drive to The Willows, Mrs. Haworth was chatting about the rules and activities at the home. Once they arrived, they pulled up to the back of building. "I have seen photos of The Willows with the portico and columns, but those must have been long gone before I was there in the mid-60s."

They entered the back door and went straight to Mrs. Haworth's office. As it turned out, Mrs. Haworth was the owner and had come to the airport to meet Nancy herself. "She asked me if I wanted a single or double room," Nancy said. "I took a double. After that, all the conversation was with my mother."

After they finished their conversation, Mrs. Haworth called a taxi for Nancy's mother. When it arrived, Nancy escorted her out of the building against Mrs. Haworth's protest. They went around to the back to where the taxi was waiting. Mother and daughter said their goodbyes. Nancy watched her mother be driven off and went back into the building. "When I returned inside, I got a real tongue lashing from Mrs. H," Nancy remembered. "Mrs. H is what most of us called her. I was shown upstairs to my room, a room I made home for six months."

Nancy described her room as being pleasant enough. It was a bit old fashioned though. It had two twin beds, a free-standing closet that was four feet by two feet and six feet tall, a mirror, sink, dresser, and area rug between the two beds. "My room was on the third story, facing the main street," she said. "I say the third story because we lived basically on three floors with the nursery on the fourth floor."

The basement served as the first floor and where all went for meals. Nancy had to go down two flights of steps. She only had one pair of loafers to wear. "They would go 'Clop! Clop! Clop!' going down the stairs," Nancy laughed. "There wasn't a thing I could do about it. The girls on the main floor would say 'Here comes Tinker Bell coming down the stairs again.' I didn't really associate with the girls on the main floor, and they never came up to my floor, except to go to the doctor and deliver their babies."

The second floor, or main floor, had dorm rooms with a maximum of two to a room. This floor also had the offices. The third floor had dorm rooms, a TV room, the clinic, and the rooms for labor, delivery, and recovery. The fourth floor had the babies. "There was an enclosed yard on the south where we walked, if we wanted," Nancy said, "and most of us did. So many times around the perimeter equaled a mile. We tried to walk a mile in all kinds of weather."

After settling into her room and getting her bearings, Nancy "Sandy" started her daily living at The Willows. A couple days after arriving, the social worker went to talk to her about the adoption. It wasn't counseling about alternatives, it was just questions about her and the baby's father's social and medical history. The decision had already been made. She never talked to the social worker again until after her baby was born.

Nancy said she learned early on not to get too excited about meal time. "They were generally pretty bad, very nutritious but bland as no salt or seasoning was used," she said. "That was to keep our weight gain down as the goal was for us to leave not looking like we had had a baby. It wasn't unusual for us to skip a meal now and then. They didn't worry about that unless we missed too many in a row. One girl did that and the meals started showing up in her room."

Breakfast was often skipped by Nancy as she was always oversleeping until mail call. That would wake her up. Mail call was every morning about the same time. "Mrs. H would read off all our first names over the intercom and we would go down to her office area to pick up our mail," Nancy said. "All the letters were sent to our "given" names without our last names. Mine were addressed to 'Sandy Haworth.' Sometimes packages would arrive with treats. They were certainly gobbled up quickly."

Not too long after arriving, Nancy asked if she could work in the nursery. The girls were only used to help in the nursery if they volunteered. They were paid $2.00 a day for the work. "I don't know if I actually ever got paid since the money was to be taken off my bill," she said. "I do remember that I was the only one at the time to work up there. It gave me something to do."

The nursery was on the top floor and only thing on that floor. It was very sunny and bright. Nancy didn't work every day. "They would call me over the intercom 'Sandy, you are needed in the nursery,'" she said. "It was usually in the morning and would wake me up. I would get up and go upstairs to help feed the babies."

"We would keep them all snuggled in their little bassinets and prop a bottle for them so they could get fed. It was impossible to hold each one to feed them, but we would pick them up for burping," Nancy said. "The babies were eager to have even a little bit of attention and love. The babies would just watch me and watch me." She added, "I was always happy to see an empty crib when I would go into the nursery for I knew another baby went to his or her new home."

Babies were usually adopted out within a few months. Nancy remembers feeling sorry for one little guy who was there for almost a year. They did have toys and a playpen for the little guy, and he seemed quite content. She added, "One of the nurses said they had a child for almost two years, but that was very rare."

She didn't get to work the last month of her pregnancy as she said she got too big to get around the bassinets easily. "I missed those little faces, looking up at me and smiling."

KELLEE PARR

When she wasn't working in the nursery, the rest of her day was spent reading, gossiping, watching TV, playing cards, and walking. She also did embroidery and crafts that she brought with her from home. When she ran out of supplies, she would go to the department store downtown and get some more. Nancy said she has read how girls were secluded and couldn't go out or have visitors. But when she was there, things had changed. "We were allowed to go shopping one day a week," she said. "We'd usually go in at least pairs if not groups. The Catholics girls got to go out twice as they could leave on Sundays to go to Mass."

People came and visited as well. "I remember one gal whose boyfriend came to Kansas City to visit. They left and were gone for the whole weekend," Nancy said. "My mother came to visit and took me shopping and we went for a nice lunch. We also could make phone calls, and my parents called me every Sunday night."

One interesting note about going out that Nancy noted – the girls were required to wear fake wedding rings. The girls would buy gold bands at a dime store to wear out in public. Anyone they would see of course assumed they were pregnant, married young women, and they would not be judged. "We'd put on our wedding bands and call a cab. We would usually go to what we called the Hallmark Mall. I preferred to go downtown to the older big stores since I found bookstores and sewing craft projects there to buy," Nancy noted. "One thing for sure, we always ate something when we went out."

The Willows had old clothes left from past Willows' girls. The current residents could choose from these and swap out as they grew in size. "I was lucky," Nancy said. "My mother came for a visit and took me shopping so I didn't have to wear hand-me downs."

The entire time she was there she only had one roommate, even though the roommate was there only one and half months. "She came in not looking like she was pregnant. Then – boom – she relaxed, and she was eight months along," Nancy laughed. "She was from New Jersey, and we had a good time together."

Nancy and her roommate decided to rearrange the furniture in their room. "We got reprimanded, but we liked it," she said. "It stayed that way until my roommate went into labor then the housekeepers put it back their way."

At most there were only thirty or forty girls when Nancy was there. The cottages and any other buildings around the main building from earlier days were gone. Nancy remembers there was a girl from Chicago who was a Playboy Bunny, a flight attendant, and there was a school teacher. "But most of us were college girls from middle-class families. There was a fourteen-year-old girl from Tennessee there," Nancy said. "She was quite chubby and never looked pregnant. She didn't change even after she delivered."

One girl was from Minnesota and was really rich. "She stayed in her room most of the time. She's the one who skipped meals from time to time," Nancy said. "But she was fun, so we all gathered in her room to play cards and talk. She organized a bridge tournament with three tables of players. Hard to imagine girls our age playing bridge today."

The girls would visit a doctor regularly. Their names would be called out over the intercom to go to the clinic to be checked out. The further along the girls were, the more often they would need to go. "The labor, delivery, and clinic rooms were on the same floor I was on," Nancy said. "Only they were toward the back of the building. It must have been pretty sound proof, as I don't remember ever hearing anyone in pain. We also never received any massages like they talk about in the early days."

Nancy went on to say she didn't remember ever hearing that any girls had C-sections. She assumes there must have been some though. After delivery, the girls went to the recovery area for a few days before going home. "All our belongings would already be there," she said. "The other girls would come to visit to see how it all went and marvel at how thin we were and how well we looked."

She went on to say that she got to see her baby after delivery. "I was only allowed to see my child for about an hour, only once," Nancy said, "to hold him and give him a lifetime of love – just one hour."

While in recovery, the social worker would come to get the girls to take them to court. "We didn't talk much about the proceedings on the way there," Nancy said. "It would have been nice to know what it was going to be like. We would sit at a large table with men and women around it asking us questions as to why we were giving up our child. Tough questions. I think, in retrospect, it didn't matter what I said since it was pretty much a 'done deal.' This was just a formality. We signed the papers and went back to the home."

Nancy shared that the social worker did ask her if she wanted to know what kind of people adopted her baby. "Of course. Yes, please. I would appreciate it!" Nancy said. "She said she would write and let us know. I got a letter about a month later about the adoptive parents. They were a wonderful couple. The father had a good job, and the mother was a Sunday School teacher. Funny how one of my friends wrote to me that she had gotten her letter about her baby's family, too. It was – wonderful couple, good job, Sunday School teacher. It read exactly like the one I received. Hmmmmmm."

The Sunday after she'd gone to court to relinquish her son, Nancy's parents called. She told them she was ready to go home and come get her. When they arrived, they told her they had made reservations at a spa some place in Missouri. "They said they needed to whip me back into shape," Nancy said chuckling. "But that I looked better now than when I went in."

Nancy wanted to emphasize that The Willows was not a prison. The nurses and housekeepers were all very nice to them. The girls formed bonds with each other. "We cared for each other," she said. "But other than her friend writing to describe the adoptive parents, we never corresponded. We never knew each other's last names."

MANSION ON A HILL

"I do feel sad such institutions aren't around anymore," Nancy lamented. "There are just a few today. Abortions and more single mothers keeping their babies seem to be the way now. However, there are so many couples wanting babies, The Willows would have been a good source for them."

Nancy always hoped one day she would meet and get to know her son, Chad. She never went looking for him as she felt it was not right for her to interrupt his life. If he wanted to find her, she would love to meet him but didn't actively search herself. She did put her information out to find her if he did ever come looking. She posted information on the International Soundex Reunion Registry (ISRR), adoption.com, and a couple other adoption sites she discovered over time.

In September of 2018, her dream came true. She was vacationing in Branson, Missouri, with family when she got a text message. "I think I'm your son."

"He was my son, and it has been wonderful," Nancy said.

The reunion took place a few months later over New Years. Nancy said, "Oh my goodness, I have to interject a funny story. I always had a mental image of Chad, who his adoptive parents named Jeff. I thought he probably looked like my son, Sean – about same height, same hair, etc. So, when they came to visit over New Years, I had this all played out in my mind. I was going to say 'My you've grown since I last saw you.'"

"I opened up the door, and there was Stephanie, my granddaughter. We hugged. And then I saw Brandon my grandson and my son's wife Kimberly. We hugged and she was crying. Then Chad was standing behind them. He was just as tall as they were, but he wasn't standing on the top step yet. He turned out to be 6'5". When I went to hug him, I said, 'Oh my, you did grow from the last time I saw you!' It just blew my mind, and we just laughed."

Nancy said she always knew they would change her son's name because she herself was adopted, and her name was changed. Chad's name was changed to Jeff, and he is Jeff to her today. Going through the whole process of reuniting can be awkward and difficult opening up to share past history. The fact Nancy was adopted, found her birth mother, and learned her history helped her understand the emotions in an adoption reunion.

Jeff shared with Nancy that when he was looking for her, he saw the name Chad. He had a memory of his mother telling him the story of how they went to get him at The Willows. He would ask her "Tell me the story of when you went to get me." His mom told him the nurse handed him to her and said, "I would like for you to meet your new son, Chad."

He always remembered the name Chad and that was the link he needed to find her. Nancy said they had three wonderful days together on their first visit to get to know one another. They have stayed close in touch. Kimberly and Stephanie were coming for a week over the summer to visit for a girls' week. It has been a wonderful reunion.

Chapter 22

Danielle's Story
(1969)

Thanks to The Willows' Facebook group, I was able to meet Danielle. She shared with others in the group about her tireless search for her biological mother. She never gave up, and the reward was great. Danielle was born in the last year The Willows was open. Her story is heartwarming.

Let me begin by saying, both my biological mother and I were born at The Willows. Yes, I know this is quite an unusual situation. But you can see The Willows played a huge part in my life. I was born in 1969 and my biological, or bio, mother in 1949. I have known for as long as I can remember that we were both born at the same place because my adoptive parents told me, but I could not remember if it was The Willows or at the Florence Crittenden home.

I thought about my biological or bioparents my whole life. I was never fully convinced that I wanted to know them as people, but I always wanted to see them. Growing up, people often told me how much I looked like my mom or how much my brothers and I looked alike. I would always silently think/scream to myself, "I don't look like these people. I can't look like them. I don't know who I look like." Sometimes I would tell people that we were not blood-related or that I was adopted and sometimes I would just let go.

My adoptive mother passed when I was 19 years old. She always said that she would help me find my biological parents if I wanted to. She would tell me the details that she knew about them periodically over the years. It was hard for me to begin my initial search because I felt like it was a betrayal. It was something she and I were going to do together one day. But I think she would be happy that I went forward.

Over the years, I only told a few people that I was interested in searching and rarely mentioned all of the adoption groups and websites where I had signed up. I never told my adoptive dad or brothers about my search until 2016 when I ordered my first DNA test and my non-identifying information. I felt like I needed them to know before I got too far into the search that I was convinced this would be the last one. Interestingly, my adoptive dad is also adopted. While I thought he would be the least supportive person imaginable, he surprised me with his support. He knew all about the recent changes to Missouri's adoption law and had even considered ordering his certified copy of his original unamended birth certificate. He wished me luck and even asked me along the way how my search was going. Months later, I would help him fill out his request for his birth certificate.

In December 2016, I requested my non-identifying information from the courts in Jackson County and it confirmed I was born at The Willows. Most of what I was told as a child by my adoptive parents was confirmed by this information. Additionally, I received a lot of details about my bioparents that I had not been told. Somehow someone missed redacting my biomother's first name in two places. It took me a second to realize what I was reading. I had to reread that section a couple times to digest the fact that her first name was on the paper. Suddenly, I felt like my bioparents were real people – not just random facts but actual people. They had hobbies and interests with jobs and feelings of their own. So, I set about my search in earnest for the umpteenth time to actually find them.

MANSION ON A HILL

Next, I submitted a DNA sample to one of the big three testing companies. From the DNA test, I did not find any close relatives, but I did find over 2,000+ distant cousins. It was a bit overwhelming, but I checked my matches regularly hoping for clues.

About the same time that I ordered by non-identifying information, I came across a searcher who told me she knew someone who had access to the Missouri birth index. She contacted her friend and soon gave me the name of the woman whom she identified as my birth mother. Not knowing the searcher or this other mysterious person, I was unsure whether to trust the information. However, when I read the name given on the non-identifying information, the first name matched what the searcher told me.

Armed with my non-identifying information and a name, I was able to get support from a website called G's Adoption Registry. They provide help for adoptees searching. Very soon, the search angels at G's started sending me information on all the women in Missouri with that name. Unfortunately, it is a fairly common name. After my going through a long list of names with no luck, one night one of the searchers emailed me and asked if I had looked at a particular woman in Kansas. She included a number of facts about her and her immediate family members. I knew instantly this was my biological mother. This was March 17, 2017, a day I will always remember.

The next day my biological mother and I made contact. We first sent instant messages and then a few days later spoke by phone. (Because I want to respect her privacy, I will refer to my biomother as BB.) In our first conversation, BB told me that she had very little to say in the decision to give me up for adoption – and this was often the case with unmarried pregnant women at that time. Her parents took her to The Willows because that is where they had adopted her. She told me that she and the other girls were kind of scared. Mostly it was because they were not well versed in what to expect, but also The Willows was kind of a dark creepy old house. She said they were treated nicely by the staff. She was there from November until I was born in January. While she was at The Willows, my biological father visited her.

After I was born, The Willows' staff only let BB hold me for about an hour. It breaks my heart to know that was it. So, for 48 years, we had only that one hour. I can only imagine how hard it must be to hold your baby for such a short time, knowing that it will be the only time.

I do not know if my biofather ever saw me. BB told me the name of my biofather during our first few texts, and we both soon discovered that he died March 15, 2007. I have located several members of his family, but at this time I only have limited contact with one of his sisters. He had one son and raised his step-daughter.

Through BB and my conversations, we decided to start searching for her biological parents. BB's adoptive parents left a few documents in their safe, which she found after they died. The documents contained the name of her biomother as well as BB's original given name. Luckily, both names were very unusual, and in a short time we had identified the woman we believed to be her mother. BB decided to do a DNA test. Nothing too exciting showed up initially. So, she did another one with a different company. Lo and behold, she had a half-brother who had tested unbeknownst to us. All of the major DNA testing companies provide testers with a list of their DNA matches, along with either a way to contact them within that particular website or in some cases with an email address. We decided to wait a few days and see if he contacted her first. He didn't so BB sent him a lengthy email via the testing site telling him who she was and how they were connected. A few days later, he emailed her via a different online genealogy site without referencing her initial email. After a few emails back and forth and conversations with other members of the immediate family, he was convinced that BB's documentation proved who she was. He was indeed her younger brother. And more importantly, it proved who BB's mother and my grandmother was.

MANSION ON A HILL

BB's mother was a single woman from a prominent family in North Carolina. Her sister, a nurse, helped her to find The Willows in late 1948 before she was too far along. From BB's non-identifying information, it seemed as though BB's father married her mother shortly after she returned to North Carolina. However, the DNA test and subsequent tests of two other half-siblings disproved that the man she married is BB's biofather. We were fairly convinced we would never know BB's father's identity.

In March of 2018 barely a year later and with the help of a second cousin whom we also found through DNA, we have now identified BB's father, my grandfather. We were able to get consent for a DNA test from my presumed grandfather's son. The results have just been posted, and we have confirmed that he is in fact BB's father, my grandfather. It's pretty unbelievable when I think about it – after searching on and off for nearly 20 years, in the span of a year and a half, I have an entire family tree.

In my first phone conversation with BB, I told her that I wanted to know my health history and if she would not mind, I would like to have a photo of her. I would have understood if she did not want any further contact, but I wanted to know what she looked like. I had to see her.

As I write this I am choked up because being able to see her ended up being more important to me than I even imagined. I think as adoptees we stuff our feelings down for fear of rejection. I knew it would be an emotional thing for me, but honestly, I wasn't prepared for the love that I have received from her or that I feel for her. We are so much alike. We look alike, we have similar interests, and we have had a number of similar life experiences. Seeing someone that you look like for the first time is really profound. I do not know how to describe it because it is still completely foreign to me.

BB and I met in December 2017 when I was in Kansas from Florida for the holidays. My husband and I spent the better part of one day visiting with BB at her home. I could not stop staring at her. It was like visiting with someone I had known for years. We talked about so many things – growing up, our interests and hobbies, our families, our life experiences.

During our visit, one of her friends stopped by to check on her (or maybe to check up on me and make sure the visit went well). After her friend left she mentioned that she had told her circle of friends that I was coming to meet her. Up until then, we had not discussed whether she had told anyone about me. Honestly, it just did not matter to me because I understand that most women were pressured into keeping adoption a secret. I felt that it was her decision and her secret to tell or not tell. I still feel like I need to protect that privacy for her – so while I am sharing *our* story, I feel the need to maintain some sense of discretion for her at the same time.

After we left that day, my husband remarked on how close we were for all the years that I lived and worked in that area. Our paths could have crossed at any time. I told him that I often would look into a crowd of people and wonder if my parents were in the sea of faces.

My other link to The Willows is that one of my two adopted older brothers was born there. He says he has no interest in searching for his biological parents. He was born in October 1965 to a woman who travelled to The Willows from the east coast. Our parents shared details of what they knew with him, as they did with me. I don't know if he will ever decide to search, but I fear he may never get to know his full story if he waits too long to look. It is of course, his choice and I truly respect that. We all must follow our own journey without regret. My other adoptive brother, who passed in 2003, was adopted through a different home in the Kansas City area.

As you can see, adoption has touched my family in many ways (and in more ways than I have included here). Everyone's experience is as unique as they are, but I can say that the journey has been worth it for me. My relationship with my birth mother will be its own unique rela-

MANSION ON A HILL

tionship, and I look forward to seeing where it takes us. Whatever happens, I am very thankful to have had the opportunity to meet her and know her.

Chapter 23

The Rest of Leona's Story

Leona was a perfect example of the many women who passed through the door of The Willows. She went on to live a happy life but never forgot the daughter she left behind in Kansas City when she boarded the train to go home. Without a doubt, she would say she led a pretty uneventful life, but I found her life quite remarkable. This is the rest of her story.

Grams passed away not too long after Leona arrived home. Leona would later say that 1925 was the saddest year of her life. She lost her baby and her grams that year. She could hardly bare it.

Leona stayed with her mama on the farm. A few weeks after returning home, Leona and Goldie made the trip by foot into Havana to go to the general store for supplies that Mama needed. It was a spring Saturday, similar to the day Leona walked with Goldie to the dance and met Nick for the first time. Memories flooded back as they walked through the blossoming apple orchard. How life had changed. Leona felt it would never be the same. Goldie walked arm-in-arm with her and tried to cheer Leona up by singing "Toot, Toot, Tootsie, Goodbye." Goldie could carry a tune no better than Leona, and the two started laughing. It was a healing laugh. The rest of the way into town the two sang at the top of the lungs every song they could think of to sing.

One of the hardest things for Leona upon returning home was the fear of running into Nick or Mr. Belt. Thankfully Havana was quite a distance from Hale, and if the Belts went to a bigger town for goods, they probably went to Longton or Sedan. Leona never did see or hear from them again. Apparently for them it was as if the "little problem" never happened. However, several months after Leona returned to the farm, Goldie brought home a Sedan newspaper from town. She ran to Leona and showed her the folded paper with the notice that Nick's wife had filed for divorce. Leona said she tried to not be too gleeful over it but had to admit she felt he deserved it.

Leona turned eighteen the next December. The following summer she met a handsome man named Russell, and they began dating. It was so difficult for Leona to date. The guilt of her past and giving up her baby Marcia would never go away. She had been told at The Willows that this was a new beginning for her, but it was so hard to forget. She also was told she shouldn't tell anyone about her past "situation" because knowing would cause people to look down on her. But she couldn't hide the truth from Russell. She told Russell about Nick and having been at The Willows. Russell wiped the tears from her eyes. He said, "Leona, what is in the past is in the past, and we won't ever talk about this again. I love you now."

When he asked her to marry him, Leona had to be honest with Russell about what she was feeling. She told Russell she loved him, but if she couldn't have her Marcia, she didn't want to have any children at all. Without even blinking, Russell told her he loved her, and it didn't matter. He was fine if they didn't have children as long as he had her, and they never did. The young couple were married on July 27, 1928.

Leona and Russell's Wedding Photo
July 27, 1928

It was tough making a living on the farm. Shortly after Leona was married, Louis took off, heading west to find a job. He found work in Oregon, building the roads around Crater Lake. He wrote to Leona and Russell and said there were jobs there. They should come join him. It was a difficult decision to leave home, but Goldie and Bud were still there to look out for her mama. In September of 1928, Leona and Russell took the train to Portland, Oregon, to meet Louis.

Russell and Leona had no idea what their lives would be like when they headed to Oregon on the train. She felt like it was the new start she'd been told to expect, but the train ride brought back the nightmare trip to Kansas City with Louis. She pushed the memories of baby Marcia out of her mind. She was glad Russell was with her. He could sense her tension and held her close. The trip took several days as they crossed half the country. It was exciting and terrifying at the same time. So many people were headed west. What if the job didn't pan out like Louis promised? What if they hated life in Oregon and missed Kansas?

Louis ran up and threw his arms around his baby sister when she arrived at the train depot. He swung her around with glee while Leona laughed. Russell and Louis shook hands, grabbed the bags with all of their possessions, and Louis led them to his car. The men loaded the bags, and they all climbed in. Louis was so excited to have family there. He also had some news. He had met a gal. Her name was Ruby. He couldn't wait for them to meet her. He had a smile on his handsome face that told Leona that Louis was in love. She had never seen him so giddy.

They headed south from Portland on the long drive to the work area around Crater Lake. Leona was struck by the beauty of the landscape, the mountains and huge trees. A far cry from the Kansas landscape with rolling hills and short hedge trees around their farm. Louis started telling them about the jobs he had lined up for them. The work was hard, but it paid pretty good considering the difficult times.

Leona never shared too much about their work experience other than that the living conditions were very rough, especially in the winter. They worked for Orman Road Construction. She herself to be one of the few women on the road construction crew. Leona said the crew had a large tent for meals and to socialize together after long hours of work. The men would play cards, smoke and tell tall tales of hunting and fishing. Leona and Russell first lived in a small tent, but eventually they were able to buy a silver streamline trailer house. All the workers camped in the same campground with their trailers. Years later, after Leona heard of the death of a man they had worked with, she wrote in a letter, "He was seventy-nine years old. Our friends, men especially, are about all gone. Guess women are tougher than men. Haha! Maybe we don't work as hard."

One of Leona's first trips to see the ocean

Leona and Russell loved living in Oregon. They loved the mountains and going to the coast to see the ocean. It was also a perfect place for hunting and fishing. The couple shared this passion their entire married life. "I loved to hunt and fish," Leona said. "I even trapped possums and skinned them to sell their hides." She laughed, "I even skinned a skunk once. Didn't smell good and neither did I."

MANSION ON A HILL

Louis and Leona early hunting trip

Russell and Leona with their game

In 1944 Leona got word her sister passed away, leaving two small children. She and Russell took her niece and nephew in. They became her children to raise. She told Russell they couldn't live in a trailer with two children so they bought their first home in Klamath Falls, Oregon. She was so happy to have a real house of her own. It was the first time since she was a teen she felt she had roots.

When her nephew was older, he started to get into a little trouble with the crowd he was running around with at school. Russell came home one day and told Leona he had bought a farm outside Dorris, California, so they could get their boy into a better environment. He had sold the house to buy the farm and had quit construction work. Leona was livid. She loved her home. To make matters worse, the farm was located in the sandy hills where hardly anything grew, and the little house was a shack in comparison to Leona's city house. They had no running water or indoor bathroom. It was a far cry from the life she had become accustomed to living.

Leona had to agree though that it was the best decision for her nephew and their family. After lots of weeding, cleaning fields, picking up rocks, and slowly fixing up the house, she began to enjoy their farm. They had lots of elk to hunt and great places to fish nearby. It was a life she loved.

The children grew up and moved away from home. Age was catching up with Russell and so was farm life. One day he came back from town and again surprised Leona. He told her he had sold the farm and bought a house in town. How could he sell their farm? She didn't want to move to town! There was no arguing with the man though. Leona packed her bags once again, and they moved into Dorris into the house where they lived the rest of their lives. As she said years later, "He used a down payment of the farm to buy this current house, and we just stuck with it."

Russell passed away in December of 1977 at the age of seventy-one. Leona remained living alone in their little house. She planted beautiful flowers around the house. She had fruit trees and a large garden to grow vegetables. Every year she canned all the produce she grew and cut wood to burn in the fireplace to last the long snowy winters. She kept on hunting and fishing as long as her bum knee wasn't too sore from arthritis. She enjoyed her extended family living close by. Her brother Bud and his wife lived outside Dorris. She had lots of nieces, nephews, and great nieces and nephews. She loved to cook and bake. She always had some baked goods ready to share. Her family would often stop by for some of her pineapple upside-down cake or a piece of fresh baked apple pie. She felt she had a blessed life. All except for the secret she carried since she was seventeen. She still wondered where her Marcia might be.

She thought often of her little girl, now a grown woman. Had her mother bought her a doll? What did she look like now? Was she married? Had she had a good life? Questions that crossed her mind so often. Valentine's Day was hard. She never liked that day. When her nephew had a boy born on February 14, it brought her joy and pain. Every year after his birth she baked him a cake. However, in her heart it was also for her Marcia.

Then on a warm summer day in 1991, Leona received a letter in the mail. It was from her home state of Kansas. She didn't recognize the return address. She opened the letter. Her whole body shook with excitement and fear as she read. It was from a young man asking if she might be the Leona May who had given birth to a baby girl on Valentine's Day 1925 in Kansas City, Missouri. His mother was this baby girl, who was born at The Willows, and he was looking for her birth mother.

Leona knew the minute she began reading the letter that her life would forever be changed. The secret she had kept for so long was about to be revealed – if she responded. She didn't know if she wanted to answer or not. It was a little frightening. She didn't know what to do. What would people think of her? She didn't think she wanted anyone from Dorris to know about her past.

More than once she reread the letter contemplating what she should do. At night she tossed and turned. Leona thought about the words she had read in the letter. Her daughter had enjoyed a wonderful life. She was married and lived on a farm in Kansas. She had three children, two girls and a boy. "Oh my, I have grandchildren," Leona realized.

The next day Leona called her niece Lola, the one who had been at the train station to greet her with sister Iva after Leona left The Willows. Leona had always assumed Lola had known about baby Marcia. When Leona asked Lola what she thought she should do, Lola was caught totally by surprise. She had no idea Aunt Ona had ever had a baby. Leona gave Lola a little history of her long-kept secret. After Leona shared her dilemma and mixed emotions, Lola gave her aunt some sage advice. "Aunt Ona, they have reached out to you, and you need to share with them about yourself because you're a sweet and special lady," she said. "You deserve to know about your daughter and grandchildren. Absolutely, I think you should write them back."

Leona took the entire next day writing and rewriting her letter with her shaky handwriting. She kept considering the consequences. Memories she had long tucked away of The Willows and her baby came flooding back. She folded her letter and stuffed it in the plain white envelope. After carefully copying the address, she added a stamp and headed out the door before she lost her nerve. It was a short walk to the post office. Leona felt anxious and almost turned around. Was she doing the right thing? She kept going. Entering the little brick building, she waved to her friend the postal clerk she had known for years. Leona couldn't help but pause, wondering what her old friend would think of her if she knew what was in this letter. The mail drop was just a step away. Leona moved toward the slot, gave the letter a little kiss, and dropped it into the mail.

MANSION ON A HILL

Author's Note

A few years ago, I found hundreds of letters Leona wrote to my mother. Yes, Leona was my grandmother. She was eighty-three years old, and my mother was sixty-six. Leona had fourteen years to get to know her long lost daughter.

After reading my grandmother's letters, I learned about details the two shared with one another as they developed their new mother/daughter bond. I knew I needed to document their lives and reunion story for my family. This led to my book My Little Valentine. *It tells the tale of the search and divine intervention (or just plain good luck) in reuniting. This journey led me to begin my research on The Willows and meeting some incredible people along the way.*

Thank you to all my family and friends who have encouraged me to tell the rest of Leona's story and the history of The Willows. Thank you also to those who have shared their Willows' stories with me. There are hundreds of these wonderful reunion stories and more happening every day now that the Missouri laws on original birth certificates have changed. I would love to hear from others and their reunion stories. Maybe another book could be in the making.

I hope you have enjoyed Mansion on a Hill, *and for those still searching for birth parents or children, I encourage you to keep searching and never give up hope to find your answers.*

Bibliography

[1] Scheuerman, D. (2007, November/December). Lost Children: Riders on the Orphan Train. *Humanities,* 28.

[2] *The Sun Tribune,* July 2, 1950.

[3] Haworth, E. P. (1925 The Sanitarium publisher). "Who Enter Here Find Quiet and Peace and Rest."

[4] Haworth, E. P. (1924, Empire Ptg. Co. publisher). "Finesse of Service: Explaining to Our Physician Patrons Some of the Refinements in Our Plans for the Protection of Their Unfortunate Patients."

[5] Haworth, E. P. (1917, The Sanitarium publisher) "The Willows Maternity Sanitarium Catalogue."

[6] Kansas City Public Library (1909) Photo: The Willows Maternity Sanitarium.

[7] *The Kansas City Star,* December 24, 1908.

[8] *Medical Review* (1907, Advertisement) "The Willows Maternity Sanitarium."

[9] Haworth, E. P. (1930 and 1937, The Sanitarium publisher). "A Ten Years' Survey of Seclusion Maternity Service: A Sociological Analysis of the Patients Cared for by The Willows Maternity Sanitarium Covering the Ten-year Period, 1920–1929 Inclusive."

[10] Haworth, E. P. (1917, The Willows Maternity Sanitarium publisher) "My Diary by Elizabeth."

[11] Haworth, E. P. (1918, The Willows Maternity Sanitarium publisher) "By-Paths and Cross-Roads: Accidents of Fair Travelers on the Highway of Life."

[12] Haworth, E. P. (1927, The Sanitarium publisher) "Who Will Help – How to Get Help."

[13] *The Kansas City Star*, July 15, 1969.

[14] Haworth, E. P. (1925, The Willows Maternity Sanitarium publisher) "Basis of Estimating the Charges for the Care of a Patient at the Willows Maternity Sanitarium."

[15] *Lawrence Journal-World*, June 21, 1975.

[16] Haworth, Mrs. E. P. (1930, The Willows Maternity Sanitarium publisher) "Baby Bares."

[17] *The Kansas City Star*, December 16, 1934.

[18] *San Antonio Light*, November 8, 1925, "Like a 'Vamp' in the Movies – Startling Exploits and Experiences in the Restless Career of Lydia Locke, Who Shot One Husband, Divorced Two, Plotted With a Bogus Baby and Is Before the Courts Once More." p. 8.

[19] *The Washington Post*, November 11, 1924.

Born and raised in Kansas, KelLee now lives in Manhattan, Kansas, where he enjoys the beauty of the Flint Hills. Besides writing, he enjoys gardening, hiking, and Kansas State sports.

Made in the USA
Monee, IL
09 August 2023